THE STORY OF IMMORTALITY

A RETURN TO SELF-SOVEREIGNTY

THE STORY OF IMMORTALITY

Inspired by
Mohini Panjabi

Special Contribution of Afterword
Dadi Janki

Research
Rita Cleary
Julia Grindon-Welch
Erik Larson
Veronica McHugh
Steve Naraine

Editorial
Carol Gill
Gayatri Naraine
Judy Rodgers

Design
Emily Owen
Ruder Finn Print, a Division of Ruder Finn, Inc.

Illustrations
Atanu Roy

Cover Art
Sigrun Olsen

To all those who contributed to the making of *The Story of Immortality* —
our heartfelt thanks.

Copyright © 2008 Brahma Kumaris World Spiritual Organization (USA)
Global Harmony House
46 South Middle Neck Road
Great Neck, NY 11021
516.773.0971
www.bkswu.org

ISBN: 978-1-886872-51-6

Printed in China by Everbest through Four Colour Imports Ltd., Louisville, Kentucky

DEDICATED TO

RAJAYOGINI DADI PRAKASHMANI

TO MY LONG-LOST CHILDREN

TABLE OF CONTENTS

FOREWORD

All cultures in the world have myths and fairy tales about heroes and heroines who set out on a search for lost treasure or a lost kingdom. Their journey requires them to face obstacles, learn lessons, and pass tests until finally, one day, they are victorious: their lost treasure is found, their kingdom reclaimed. There is a reason that we thrill to these stories in all of their many different renditions. It is because they are our story.

These fairy tales and myths describe the spiritual journey of each soul through its experience on earth. The treasures lost are the spiritual wealth with which a soul enters the world, and the throne relinquished is the state of self-sovereignty that belonged to each soul when it first entered the world from the soul world. The story of the souls in time is a story of the loss of our original greatness and eventually even the forgetting that we were great, until one day – utterly disoriented and on the brink of despair – we are lucky enough to find a hidden door that takes us onto a path of ascent that was invisible before.

Today the world is filled with people wandering in search of something – some are searching for truth, some are searching for God. Always it is a search for a true identity – an explanation of who they really are and where they fit into the vast story of humanity.

My own quest began in India, where I was born, and eventually took me to a source of deep spiritual knowledge that is still relatively unknown, though it has touched the lives of hundreds of thousands of seekers throughout the world. The knowledge was originally given orally from one person to another and is still given that way, carefully allowing each one to understand what is being said. While it is a path that leads directly to God's door, it is not a path of devotion – there is no chanting or supplications. It reveals a body of knowledge through which the Father of all souls explains to His children, the souls – the spirits living within the bodies – who they really are, where they really came from, and what they must do at this time to reclaim what they have lost. It is a story that explains the immortality of the soul and its remarkable return journey back to its original state of self-sovereignty. It is a spiritual study and practice that awakens the soul and shows each one how to prepare for the extraordinary transition that is about to occur in the world.

Over the 45 years I have studied this knowledge, it has brought me and those who are studying with me a joy greater than anything we have experienced through our senses. As I studied this knowledge, the stories of the different faiths began to fit together into a coherent whole. It was clear that many religions had a piece of the larger puzzle, an account of the story of the souls in the world told from the perspective of their religious founder and their religious clan. Not only is there a joy in understanding, but just as in the tales of knights of old or beggars who turn out to be princes, there is the gaining of a mastery of the deeper talents and arts of life that — when tested — show one's true mettle. As the body and mind are mastered, the evils of the world shrink away and the hero is not only a sovereign, but is also able to be a benefactor to others in need.

It is my joy of discovery and deep gratitude that inspired me to want to share this knowledge in a written form, in a book that could be made available to others who are searching the world for the seminal story that unlocks the disjointed mixture of fact and fiction that historians, scientists, and writers of sacred texts have pieced together.

I gathered a team of those who are also studying this spiritual knowledge to help in this task. For over a year we pored over transcripts of many of the oral lessons, studying the concepts and the different ways they are explained. In the second year, we began to review the research and to write drafts of the chapters. A few members of the team focused on the writing. My role was to review the chapters to see that the different aspects of the knowledge had been included accurately.

As you will see, we have threaded the study together with a tale about a seeker. It could be you, or anyone who has been stumbling around in the world, trying different paths, going to hear different masters, waiting for the experience that resonates within, saying, "Yes, this is it. This is the truth." Although the seeker's story is a tale, it is woven from the truth. The lessons she is given are written down in this book using the words and the metaphors originally used when these lessons were spoken, although they were originally spoken in Hindi. In some cases, we have retained a Hindi word, usually when we could not find an English one that worked as well. We have included notes in the glossary at the end of the book to explain words and concepts that were raised in the chapters.

When these words were originally spoken, they were spoken through a medium, a knowledgeable, spiritually-oriented man who received these teachings for over 30 years. In the original classes, which were spoken in India, the "voice" shifts from first person to third person. We have retained both voices to allow the readers to appreciate the accuracy of the spoken word. We trust this shift in voice will not be too distracting.

We have tried to make the information as accessible as possible, but the knowledge offered here is deep and nuanced. In order to take full benefit from the book, you will want to read it slowly, when your mind is clear and quiet, and you will want to read the lessons in sequence, as ideas are explained more completely when they are initially introduced. Many concepts are explained early in the book and elaborated on at a later point.

It is my hope, and the hope of everyone who worked on this book, that what you will find here will shed light on your own spiritual journey.

Mohini Panjabi

President, Brahma Kumaris
North, South, and Central America and the Caribbean

REFLECTION

When you look back now, you can see clearly the most important day, the moment . . . the instant of your life that changed forever everything that was to follow. Of course, at the time you had no way of knowing that you were on the brink of adventure. You are quite sure – although you do not remember exactly – that the most auspicious day – the day of new direction – began like every other day that preceded it . . .

*Y*ou emerge from the world of sleep into the world of waking – or what you think then is the world of waking – and move into your day. On one level you move through the routines of your day as if following a script, but on another you are constantly scanning, watching for a clue, a signal that might promise a break in what has become a numbing life. For some time you have been living with an emptiness, a loneliness, and a weariness with the world. There is a darkness and heaviness in the world that you do not recall feeling when you were young. You experience it as a loss of innocence or goodness. When did this mean-spiritedness creep into the world? It seems that greed has become more commonplace than generosity, and that so many are angry. And the sadness! It's everywhere. You sense from deep inside that this cannot be the inevitable path of the world. It is unbearable.

You wander through bookstores, into public lectures, and into spiritual settings in search of the kind of ground truth that will shed light on your life, on these times, and on what it is that you should be doing to uplift yourself and to help this struggling world. This wandering goes on for a long time, and then suddenly one day, when you least expect it, a door appears before you, and you walk through it, entering a new space and time.

This is the story of the Confluence Age, the most subtle and elevated of the great ages of humankind. However, unlike the other ages, this one is available only to those who grasp the difference between the temporal, material world and the eternal, spiritual universe that moves within it . . .

ONE

THE ELEVATED CONFLUENCE AGE: PASSAGE TO THE NEW WORLD

*I*n an auspicious moment that you do not anticipate and barely recognize when it arrives, you walk through a mysterious door that was not there only moments before, and you enter a magical chamber.

It is filled with a soft white light – as if lit by ten full moons. You instinctively slip off your shoes and take a few tentative steps across the room. As you do, your feet sink as if on down cushions or clouds. The walls seem to be made of a fluid white silky fabric. They are luminous in the light of those moons – or maybe the walls are somehow only made of light. It is the quality of the atmosphere that lets you know you have stepped away from the world. It is filled with purity and peace, seeming as familiar as home and, at the same time, like nothing you have ever experienced in your life.

At the far end of the chamber is an exquisite star – a point of light with beams radiating out from the center. Your gaze moves toward this star, gliding into its beauty and depth. It feels as if within the tiny center point of this star there is an eternity. You move toward the star, like a needle drawn to a magnet. As you get closer, the light fills your field of vision until it reaches the very edges of your visual world. In this feeling of being bathed in light, your heart opens. Whatever thoughts or burdens you were feeling before fall away, and you feel suspended in the moment. Your breathing becomes very slow: there seem to be centuries between each breath.

After a time, your eyes begin to make out the contours of a scene in front of you. Emerging from this atmosphere of light is a landscape, a place so peaceful and pure that you immediately feel safe, as if you are moving under the benevolent spell of very good omens.

Before you can fully take in the pristine landscape around you, you see that you are not alone. There is a Presence here. An older man, rather tall and nice looking, is approaching you. As He gets closer, He sees that you do not recognize Him, and He pauses just in front of you. Putting His hands together, palms flattened against each other in the area around His heart, He welcomes you with His eyes.

You stand in front of Him, unsure of what to do. Though you cannot place Him, in His steady gaze, you feel as if this is someone you have known from before memory, someone who has been waiting for you over these many years that you have been wandering, someone who is perhaps a Benefactor.

He greets you with the instant love and familiarity you have only known with family or old friends, and He invites you to walk with Him. You begin moving noiselessly along a path, looking around at the exquisite landscape on all sides. To your right there are rolling soft green hills as far as you can see, disappearing into the horizon. On the left is a meadow dancing with delicate flowers, none of which looks like flowers you know, and beyond that in the distance – a shimmering silver-blue lake. You can hear birdsongs, lilting tunes you do not know, and the air – it smells like sweet perfume. Your heart feels light and happy in the sheer beauty of this setting.

You turn your attention away from the beauty surrounding you and look at this One you are walking with. He returns your gaze. He is taller than you are, with kind brown eyes, a white mustache, and thinning white hair. You tilt your head up and look into His eyes, which are reassuring. He asks if you are tired, if you would like to stop and rest for awhile. You tell Him that it is not that you are tired physically, but that you are feeling a deep inner weariness. He understands and leads you off the path and up to a grassy area in a small grove of trees. You sit down on the grass and lean your back against a tree. He settles down near you.

He does not ask you any questions about where you have been or what brought you to this place. It is as if He knows where you have been and knew that today – this moment – was the moment when you would arrive here. He begins to tell you things that – if they are true – explain the sense of loss you have been feeling up till now.

He says that before you walked through the door of this magical chamber, you were living in a foreign land; that you have traveled far from your original home; and that slowly, over a very long time, you have lost everything – including even the memory of what you once were. He watches your face closely as He tells you this. You are looking at Him intently, trying to take in what He is telling you.

You were a sovereign, He explains, with extraordinary powers and a vast fortune. You came from a place where you only knew peace, happiness, and love, but over a long, long time you lost that elevated status and wandered into a degraded and dangerous land. As you hear these words, a sense of recognition stirs somewhere deep within, and you are seized with a longing for the beauty you once knew and the fortune you once had.

The door you entered, He explains, has brought you to a time and place with special attributes and powers. It is called the Confluence Age, and this is a subtle region of light only visible in this auspicious age. In this time, the smallest effort on your part brings immense help to you on your spiritual journey. In this time, you can acquire the ability to see the past, the present, and the future at once. In this time, you can learn to distinguish between illusion and truth. The gifts available to you at this special time are gifts that you once possessed.

He offers to teach you what you must do to reclaim what you have lost. If you will study the lessons He gives you here and apply them in your life, He says, you will reclaim the sovereignty you once had.

You wonder how this can be happening to you and worry that the space will close and the door will vanish as suddenly and mysteriously as it appeared. He tells you that this study and transformation are carried out in silence, which is the language of the original self, the soul. He assures you that as you learn to be still in silence, the mind will cooperate and your divine intellect will emerge, giving you divine insight to guide you forward. Wordlessly you accept His offer to teach you and settle in comfortably against the tree . . .

Teachings

is ending, and the day is beginning. You are standing in the unlimited. You are now standing at the Confluence Age. At this time, the world is in total darkness. When it is the darkest moment, it is also time for the first light of dawn. This time is called eternal and most auspicious. It is at this time of the first light of dawn, before the morning comes, that the Father awakens you. The night of seeking comes to an end, and the day of enlightenment begins.

This is the very short Confluence Age, the leap age, when the old is made into the new. You have come to ignite the spiritual flame of the soul and to open the third eye of enlightenment. In this age, your spiritual light becomes steady, stable, and sparkling. From just a thin line, the spiritual light increases within the soul until it becomes complete and full. This is the celebration of a new direction in life. It is the time of both farewell and congratulations. Farewell to the old and congratulations to the new. Farewell to old patterns of thinking, tendencies, and habits, and congratulations to new zeal, enthusiasm, and pure, elevated thinking. This is the age to use time and thoughts in an imperishable way and to celebrate long-lasting results.

AN AUSPICIOUS TIME:
THE SUPREME SOUL MEETS THE CHILDREN

The souls and the Supreme Soul have remained separated for a long time. It is at the Confluence Age that this very auspicious meeting takes place. This is why on meeting the children, the Father, the Supreme Soul, says: Beloved, long-lost and now-found children. It is you, the souls, who have been invoking the Father and asking Me to come. When the Father comes, time changes from ordinary to auspicious. This is the best meeting. It is a meeting through which souls are reconnected to the Supreme Soul and children remember the Father.

This meeting is taking place now! When the light of every soul is almost extinguished, the Father comes to awaken everyone. Everyone is asleep and is unconscious to the true self. The Father showers nectar and wakes up the children, that is, the souls. He opens your third eye with the nectar of knowledge, drop by drop. Each drop is an elevated version that describes His elevated directions and leads you to true self-sovereignty.

A Transitional Time

The confluence is the meeting of the beginning and the end, so the comparison between the past and the future can only be made now in this present time.

The Confluence Age is the passage of time through which you have to cross from one shore of the world to the other shore. Sweet child, you have now lifted your anchor from the shore of the old world and have to go across to the other shore of the new world. On one side is the salty channel of the old, sorrowful world, and on the other side is the sweet channel of a whole new world. You have your back toward the past. Past is past. Do not worry about the past but continue to move forward. You must not look back. To look back is to hang onto the things of the past. Attachments to this old world now have to be removed. You now face the future as you are moving toward the new world. You must now have just the one elevated desire of going to the land of happiness. Your true nature of peace, purity, and joy are now coming alive, and your old habits of worry, fear, and confusion are dying.

The Confluence Age is a short age to make this journey. You are now within calling distance of the new world. You can almost see the trees of your new land. To be within calling distance means that the destination is clear and definite. It is just in front of you. It is as if you just have to take one step forward, and you will reach toward that side. Now that you know that you are within calling distance of your destination, why should you step back? You must continue to step forward.

You must not come to a standstill anywhere. Do not look around anywhere. Continue to move forward and continue to face one direction, for only then will your vision become stable and your faith in your destination become unshakeable. All around this passage, times are very rough and conditions are very bad. A great deal of silent introspection is required to cross through this short passage of time. Even if you do look back, you must remain very stable. You have to remain very cautious that the rough times and bad conditions do not cause storms in your mind and do not turn your head around and take you in the wrong direction. There are many storms that will attempt to pull you out of this passage. However, the storms may try to rock the boat of your mind, but when you are stable and unshakeable, you will not drown. Just do not forget your destination!

A Transformational Time

Child, now that this old world is about to be transformed, your attention has to be on the new world. The world is one. It is new and then becomes old. It is this same old world that has to become new. You have to live here in this old world, but your intellect understands that this old world is to be transformed. Your intellect has to break the connection to the old world and be connected to creating the new world. The Father has now come to give you the gifts of a divine intellect and spiritual vision.

The divine intellect is a loving one that takes power directly from God. With this power the intellect wakes up to the knowledge of the beginning, the middle, and the end of the whole world. The divine intellect is broad, unlimited, and far-reaching. It is like a clean and pure vessel that holds the nectar of knowledge in an unadulterated way. It has the capacity to understand the subtleties of each point of knowledge and to discern truth from falsehood.

It is at this time that you receive true and pure love. Transformation cannot take place with force. Love is the power to enable transformation to take place — transformation of consciousness, of relationships, and of characteristics, that is, of attitude, habits, outlook, and actions.

It is the power of love that makes children belong to the Father. This power of love makes everything easy. When you become merged in love and use your divine gifts, you experience any difficult situation to be very easy. I also tell you to remain merged in Me, the Ocean of Love. Spiritual love is the canopy of protection under which no shadow of illusion and ignorance can exist.

An Elevated Time

The Confluence Age is called the Diamond Age because time has the highest value now. It is at the present time that you can become as valuable as a diamond. You are becoming the most elevated, the highest-on-high being. It is here, in the elevated Confluence Age, that children become self-sovereigns by studying *Raja Yoga*. Self-sovereignty is created through imbibing spiritual knowledge. Spiritual knowledge becomes your natural nature, and you naturally perform elevated actions. By telling you this, the Father gives the child the respect of being a self-sovereign.

To be a self-sovereign means to be a king of the senses, your subjects. Does the king rule, or do the subjects rule? You are able to know this, are you not? If it is the rule of the subjects, you cannot be called a king. Even if only one of the senses deceives you, you cannot be called a self-sovereign. It is at this time that by becoming self-sovereigns, you become living models of the heirs to the kingdom of the world.

This is the elevated time when human beings have the chance to ascend in their spiritual aspirations and make the impossible possible.

A Benevolent Time: The World Benefactor Gives Souls Limitless Treasures

This is the most benevolent Confluence Age. At the present time, the Father in the form of the World Benefactor benefits the whole world by giving souls imperishable, limitless treasures. At this time, you can accumulate treasures in all the accounts: the accounts of elevated knowledge, elevated powers, elevated virtues, elevated actions, and elevated relationships.

It is important to take each step recognizing the importance of this period of time, the attainments available, and the potential for accumulating. One second of this present auspicious time is so much greater than a period of ordinary time. Do you know that? Do you know clearly the account of how much can be earned in a second and how much can be lost in a second?

There are many special treasures of the Confluence Age, but the greatest treasures are the treasures of time and thoughts. Multimillions can be accumulated with every second of the Confluence Age if thoughts are used in a worthwhile way. To use the treasures of time and thoughts in a worthwhile way is to use all other special treasures at the accurate time of need.

The special treasure of knowledge brings the attainment of liberation and liberation-in-life. With understanding, the soul is liberated from all the things that give sorrow and peacelessness. You are liberated from the strings of vices that have tied you in bondage for so long. And you are released from wasteful and negative thoughts and actions. With practice, the soul is able to discern right from wrong, and you live a liberated life with enlightenment and wisdom.

The special treasure of all powers is received through the remembrance of the Father. When you have these powers with you all the time and use them to deal with the various situations and circumstances you face, then victory is guaranteed.

The special treasure of all divine virtues is the reward received from the inculcation of each point of knowledge. The specialty of each virtue is so great that it brings back spiritual vitality to your life and gives you back your beauty.

The special treasure of a generous heart is another great treasure, and it is received from doing selfless service. To use your thoughts, words, actions, and wealth in a worthwhile way in service to others brings you imperishable happiness easily and automatically.

The special treasure of blessings is received through relationships and connections. By interacting with everyone with truth, honesty, and respect, obstacles are removed; relationships become easy and free from labor; and you receive from others the blessings of trust and friendship.

The key to accumulating these treasures is not just to use them for others only, but also to use them first for the self. The attainment of the treasures makes you into an authority of experience in life. These special treasures create spiritual contentment within the soul. Contentment is called a jewel, and it puts the sparkle of spiritual intoxication on the face, which is automatically visible in every action.

A Quality Time of Silence

At the Confluence Age, everything is incognito and silent. Incognito means it cannot be seen with the physical eyes, and silent means it is not done in sound. You, the soul, are incognito. The Father, the Supreme Soul, is incognito. The knowledge is incognito, the inheritance is incognito, and your efforts and rewards are incognito. Time is silent, remembrance is silent, and transformation is silent.

You are now listening to new things. Continue to keep these thoughts in the clean vessel of your intellect, and you will experience wonders on this spiritual pilgrimage.

. . . The voice of the One who has been teaching you has come to a stop, and He is now sitting in silence next to you. He is present with you, but His attention also seems to be on something beyond . . . or maybe within. The things you have just heard are swimming in your mind. Much of it seems too subtle to grasp, but one thing is clear: This Confluence Age that your new Benefactor is describing holds great promise.

He looks at you and slowly rises to His feet. He encourages you to take some rest, and as He says this, you realize you are exhausted. You don't even remember falling asleep.

IMPLICATIONS FOR LIFE

At this blessed time of the Confluence Age,
through your one step of courage, you easily
receive multimillionfold help. Make your own
effort and attain the reward.

TWO

THE SOUL IS AN ETERNAL TRAVELER

After your first day in this new land, you sleep deeply. You have no idea for how long you sleep. It may be hours or even days. When you awaken, you are lying on a small bed under a white canopy. Someone has slipped a pillow under your head and covered you with an intricate coverlet. There is a plate of fruit on a tray next to you. The tray looks like it is woven of large green leaves of some type. You realize you are very hungry. You sit up, swinging your feet to the ground, and reach for a piece of fruit. As you do, you see that the One who welcomed you yesterday is sitting not far away. He is looking off into the distance. It appears He may be deep in thought.

As you bite into the fruit, you wonder if He has been sitting there the whole time you slept. He senses that you are awake and turns and smiles. He arises to come closer to you and inquires as to whether you have slept well. He speaks to you with so much tenderness and looks at you with so much love that you soften in His presence, assuring Him that yes, you slept very, very well. He would like to pick up His story where He left off yesterday. You are happy to do that and turn your full attention on Him as He begins to talk, fairly rapidly, again watching you intently. His steady focus and sure way of talking let you know that He feels there is something here that is important for you to understand. You sit up alert, attentive to what He is saying.

He seems to know things about you that you do not know about yourself, and you listen enrapt as He slowly reveals to you your true identity and veiled past. You are a subtle star, He tells you, an immortal and eternal traveler through time. And while you have become impure and heavy now, this is not your original nature. When you began this journey, you were as pure as gold, infused with a deep contentment and silently radiating peace. You were, He tells you, of the same quality and form as your true Father, your true Mother. You linger for a moment on this idea of your true Parent, and you wonder what this might mean.

You have been traveling in a foreign land, He says. Your original home is far, far away. It is a tower of peace and light where you used to dwell with others like yourself. Your home is a spiritual place, beyond the light and sound of the Earth plane.

You are a spirit, a form of living, conscient light, and latent within you are extraordinary powers and wondrous qualities that you are not even aware you possess.

While what He is telling you is new and strange, it seems as if you already knew this somehow . . . as if somewhere buried deep in your memory is the experience of this home, this Parent, and this spiritual family who lived there together.

He tells you that at this time, the others in this spiritual family have left the original home as well. All have traveled to the foreign land, the material world, and have become enmeshed in bodily relationships and bondages. You are all actors in a play, He explains. You have adopted bodies to play your parts, but you are only guests in these bodies. They are temporary and will age and fall away as all material things do. You are, He insists, the soul within. The body has eyes, but it is the soul that sees. The body has ears, but it is the soul that hears. When the body is wounded, it is you, the soul, who feels the pain.

This knowledge He is giving you, He says, is a study for sovereigns. If you are to reclaim your throne, you must imbibe this understanding. You were a master, but you have lost your mastery over your powers. He suggests you examine the extent to which you have ruling power over the subtle powers within you: the mind; the intellect; and the sanskars, the latent traits in the soul. These three subtle powers must cooperate with you if you are to rule your kingdom again, He counsels . . .

Teachings

you travel on this spiritual path, you
should constantly have in your awareness your eternal and original forms, as these
are the basis of your real and true identity. When the foundation of this awareness is
strong, there is definitely victory in knowing the self. While traveling along the path,
keep moving with the faith in your own experience that comes from living in the
awareness of your newly found identity. Experience is the most important treasure
on the journey of life. An experienced soul is valued as a wise person. As you travel,
learn from every moment, have faith in the benefit it offers, and accumulate it as your
experience.

The path you are traveling on is a high but easy one, and there are many side
scenes that appear along the way. Victory is to keep the destination in your awareness
and not to get sidetracked by the passing scenes. If you waste your time in looking
at trivial things, you will miss the signs along the way. Realize the importance of
this time, and travel with the companion of determination. Your destination is self-
transformation. It is a transformation in consciousness.

The moment you decide to start your journey, you receive the key of "Who am
I?" from the Father. Know how to use this key and how to take care of it. Always
keep the key with you and remember where it is. All secrets are merged in this key
of "Who am I?"

ETERNAL AND ORIGINAL IDENTITY

You, the soul, are eternal, and your role is eternal. You are real and conscious. The soul is as subtle as a star. You, the living star, are very wonderful. You are not created. You always exist as a tiny point of living light. In your eternal form, your light is fully ignited to its fullest capacity, and you live in the supreme region of light where all souls reside.

The supreme region is called the *brahm* element. *Brahm* is the element of light. Souls are distinct from the light of the *brahm* element. Just as the sun, the moon, and the stars are up above in the sky, in the same way, souls in the element of light exist there naturally without any other support. That is the pure world of natural silence, your sweet home. There, your natural state of being is of peace, purity, and bliss. You understand that all souls are the children of the one Father and that they reside with the Father in that home.

You, the soul, are incorporeal. Your original form is incorporeal. The incorporeal soul leaves its sweet home of light and enters a corporeal body. You are such an incognito tiny point, and no one knows about you. You are so absolutely subtle that you cannot be seen with the physical eyes. You can be understood, but you cannot be seen. You are so tiny that you can only be seen with the third eye of recognition.

You, the soul, are an immortal image. Each immortal soul is present on the throne of the body. You are also imperishable, and your seat is the perishable body. A soul is like an infinitely tiny point, and yet it has such a huge part within it. Because of being immortal and imperishable, you can never be destroyed, nor can your part. Every soul has its own unique part. You, the soul, cannot die; you cannot be burned or buried. Your body can.

The original form of the self should naturally stay in your awareness. Just as you are naturally able to remember your body — you do not have to practice this — in the same way, keep your original form in your awareness. In the original awareness of the soul, there is self-respect. The main attention needed is constantly to maintain your self-respect with the awareness of this original stage.

To reflect on your eternal identity and your original identity, to know yourself on those terms, and to remain in such thoughts about yourself is said to be thinking of yourself as a spiritual being. This is called the stage of soul consciousness.

THE SOUL'S INHERITANCE AT THE CONFLUENCE AGE

Each soul has a right to an inheritance from the Father. Your first inheritance is knowledge, the second is powers, and the third is divine virtues. The knowledge, powers, and virtues that are within the Father are also within you, the child. The Father makes you, the child, the master of all knowledge, powers, and divine virtues from the moment you take spiritual birth. I tell you that these are the intrinsic qualities of the self. Something that is intrinsic is a natural part of life.

Inheritance of Knowledge

The Father is a point of conscient light. That point, the self-luminous Being, the Father, is called the Ocean of Knowledge. You too are a tiny point in which all the knowledge you receive from the Father is recorded. As a soul, you are the embodiment of knowledge. Your original characteristics are those of knowledge like the Father.

Knowledge opens the third eye of the soul through which you have self-realization. It is with the power of realization that you experience yourself to be an elevated being and your original identity to be a soul.

Inheritance of Powers

Because you are a child of the Almighty Authority Father, He wills His power to you through your practice of remembrance. You are able to invoke from within yourself whichever power you need at any particular time. That is, you are able to put the power that is merged within you, the soul, into your actions in a practical form. There are eight main powers that are used by the soul in its actions: to withdraw, to tolerate, to cooperate, to accommodate, to discern, to judge, to face, and to pack up.

Inheritance of Divine Virtues

The original nature of the soul is of divine virtues. When you emerge in your awareness the treasures of your innate divine virtues of purity, peace, happiness, love, and bliss, you will be in a constant state of contentment. Any virtue you have will definitely create an impression because virtues cannot be hidden.

THE SOUL'S ENTRANCE ONTO THE WORLD STAGE

This world is a stage, and all souls are actors. This is a play about the soul and the body. You, the soul, come down here on this planet Earth from your home, in your original stage, complete with the spiritual inheritance you claimed from the Father through making efforts at the Confluence Age. You come as a soul, a being of light, and adopt a body and become a human being. Every soul has to come here on this field of action, become a human being, and play the part that is latent within through performing actions.

The role you play on Earth is contained within you and is eternally played. For example, everything is merged in a seed, and when the seed is sown in the earth, everything emerges as it grows. In the same way, when you are stabilized in the awareness of yourself as the seed form, you are in the stage of being full of all experiences. Your entire inheritance of knowledge, powers, and virtues are merged in the soul as a seed form. When the soul enters a body, its part emerges as it plays its role.

FROM SOUL CONSCIOUSNESS TO BODY CONSCIOUSNESS

When you first enter onto the world stage, you act out your part through the body in a natural state of soul consciousness. However, as time goes on, the consciousness of the soul gets mixed with the consciousness of the body, and after a while the two are considered as one. Because of this mistake, you come under the influence of illusion and ignorance. The influence of illusion and ignorance is called *maya*. As a result, you experience distress, sorrow, fear, and peacelessness. You become distant from the greatness of your life and from your true self-respect. Further, the soul is drawn to the five elements of nature as the temporary source of its peace and happiness, and the sense organs become the agent to take from this source. The soul becomes extroverted and focuses on the body, bodily relations, and bodily possessions for its sustenance and support. This limited awareness is called body consciousness.

When actions are performed in body consciousness, the soul becomes trapped by the five vices of lust, anger, attachment, ego, and greed. The original virtues and powers are suppressed by the dominance of the vices: lust overtakes purity and the spiritual powers, anger overtakes peace, attachment overtakes love, ego overtakes self-respect, and greed overtakes happiness. The influence of the five vices is called ravan. You, the soul, step down from the original seat of self-respect, and the key of "Who am I?" gets lost. You forget your true identity of being a soul, and instead, you consider yourself to be a body. You continue to play your part through the body, with each birth bringing you deeper into body consciousness. Now, once again, I am giving you the key to "Who am I?" – so listen with attention.

THE SOUL AND BODY

The incorporeal soul is imperishable, and the corporeal body is perishable. Your body does not say that the soul belongs to it; it is you, the soul, who says, "This is my body." The body is totally distinct from the soul. If there were not a soul present in the body, it would not be able to function. It would not be able to breathe. How a body is created, how a soul enters it – all of these matters are so wonderful!

A fetus of five elements is created, and then the soul comes and enters that body. The soul enters the womb four to five months after conception. When the soul enters the womb is when the mother feels movement. However, the mother is not aware of the exact time and date. That time and date of when a soul enters the womb are not recorded. It is when the child takes birth that the time and date are noted.

It is said for a soul that it is a star sparkling in the center of the forehead. The center of the forehead is the immortal throne of the soul for each human being. You, the soul, understand that when you enter your body, you sit in the center of the forehead, but you are distinct from your body.

Because your body is of a small baby, the soul is unable to speak; however, the soul is aware. There is the presence of the soul's personality and part. When your body grows a little older, you, the soul, definitely show the sparkle of what is inside of you. As the body grows, the soul remains the same size. Souls do not grow smaller or larger.

Seeing the body, you say that this one is from such and such a country, a man or a woman. You would not speak of the soul in this way. Souls do not have names, nationality, race, gender, caste, or creed. You, the soul, do not take birth in a fish or a crocodile or in 8.4 million different species. Human souls only enter human bodies. Reason also says that the birth will be according to the species: human souls in human bodies, animal souls in animal bodies.

You are a soul, and you adopt a body to play your part. After having played your part with one body, you, the soul, leave that body and take another new one and continue to play your part. The features of your body in one birth cannot be the same as in other births. The features of the body change in every birth and are unique to that particular birth. In the same way, the part a soul plays in one birth cannot be the same in its next birth. The part is specific to the birth. No one knows what he was in the past and what he will be in the future.

In one birth, some have the role of playing a part with a body for 100 years, some for 80, and some for two years. Some play a part for six months, and some die immediately at birth. Some even die in the womb before taking birth. No one's role can be the same as another's. The longest life span in one birth is 150 years. Even though souls are the same size, a tiny point, no one's body can be exactly the same as another's. Even though their life span may be the same, their personalities are different. In every birth, the relationships of souls also change.

The Soul and Sense Organs

It is the soul that does everything. It is a soul that drives this "car" that has the form of a body. Call the body a chariot or a car, it is a soul that uses it. This knowledge – that the soul does everything through the body – has vanished. The body has senses and sense organs. The soul plays its part through the physical organs. By using the sense organs of the body, you form relationships with others. When you get tired of working through your sense organs, you detach yourself from them and go to sleep. You separate yourself from your body, the sense organs become quiet, and that is called sleep.

When you are awake, your sense organs become very active. A soul needs ears, a mouth, eyes, and other organs to play its role. The immortal soul speaks through the mouth. It is the body that has eyes, but it is the soul that sees. When a soul leaves the body and you speak to the corpse, she does not answer you because she cannot hear you. If a soul is not present in a body, physical organs are no longer in use.

Your body cannot remain alive without being fed. When there is a famine, people die of starvation. It is souls, through their bodies, that eat the food. It is souls that experience the taste. It is souls that say whether it is good or bad or whether it is very delicious and has a lot of strength. When the body is wounded, the soul feels the pain. The soul says, "I am ill, I am unhappy."

There is no question of committing suicide of the soul. A soul cannot be killed; souls are eternal. It is your body through which you play your part that is killed. The body is made of the five elements. From dust to dust is said of the body, not of the soul. The soul takes the support of matter in the form of a body to play its part. When the part is over, the soul simply leaves the body and takes another.

By considering yourself to be a guest, you become free from attachment to the building of your body. Nothing belongs to a guest. A guest is given everything to use for his needs, but there is no feeling of any of it belonging to him. He will be detached and loving while using everything with attention and care. Therefore, constantly remain in the awareness of a guest, that is, a trustee of your body. The more you have the attitude of being a guest, the more elevated and cooperative the family of your sense organs will become.

After taking many births, you, the soul, are now impure, and so look at the condition of your body. Now, you and your body can become pure. This is a wonder! Therefore, you have to clean and decorate yourself with knowledge, virtues, and powers. In a soul-conscious stage, every sense organ is full of fragrance. In a body-conscious stage, there is a bad odor in every sense organ. To be someone with all powers means to be able to control all your physical senses and guide them to do whatever you want. If you want, you can make your organs work. And if you do not want them to work, you can stop them. You must be very cautious with the way you use each sense organ. The awareness of the soul has an impact on the body.

THE EYE OF RECOGNITION

It is said that the body is like a temple. Yours is a very valuable body, and so you must not be distressed by it. Recognize its value and take care of it. It is through your present body that you recognize the Father, you recognize the self, and you recognize that time is auspicious. It is in your body that you are able to transform your consciousness.

I give this advice to souls: Children, be soul conscious! Stop being body conscious! Become soul conscious and let your eye of recognition see Me, know Me, and belong to Me, the Supreme Soul. You will then be able to go beyond. There is now no strength left in souls at all. At the moment, souls are unable to go beyond the consciousness of the body and the limitations of the material world. Souls have become unhappy; they have become poverty-stricken by being stuck in these limitations. There is spiritual insolvency. Sweetest child, let your eye of recognition meet the Father's "eye." I am the One who gives you the realization that you are a soul who has equal rights to My inheritance, and this is the time to claim it.

THE SOUL AS SELF-SOVEREIGN: MIND, INTELLECT, *SANSKARS*

The mind, intellect, and *sanskars* are in the soul. The mind creates thoughts. The intellect understands and decides on the course of action. When the soul performs the actions through the sense organs, they are recorded in the soul as *sanskars*. *Sanskars* are the record of the soul's entire part.

You, the soul, are the one who makes your body work. Who are you? You are a special soul, a master almighty authority. By remaining aware of your being the master, your subtle servers of the mind, intellect, and *sanskars* will be under your control. "I, the soul, am the master of the subtle servers." This is called the stage of a self-sovereign. In this stage, your awareness is of being a master almighty authority, and your task is to rule over your main subtle servers – the mind, intellect, and *sanskars*.

As a self-sovereign, examine yourself to see the extent of your ruling power. To what extent do you have all rights over your mind, intellect, and *sanskars*? Do these subtle servers cooperate with you in ruling your self-kingdom? When these servers follow the orders that you, their master, give, then the self-kingdom runs very well.

Power of the Mind

The thinking of your mind is your first power. If your first power is accurate, then your other servers will also do everything accurately. First of all, check to see that your first server, the mind, is a constant companion of the soul, the king, and is constantly following your instructions.

Illusion and ignorance in the form of *maya* enter the mind through the doors of the senses and create many different desires. These desires trap the mind into thoughts of limited attainments. The most elevated desire of the mind is to be peaceful, and once this is fulfilled, all the other limited desires finish. Therefore, use your first power, the mind, as your special cooperative server to maintain your connection to all your spiritual rights.

It is said before you do anything, "First think!" Those who do not think before doing something or think after they have done it become an embodiment of regret. To think afterwards is to regret, and to think beforehand is the virtue of an enlightened soul. The mind is normally occupied in two types of thoughts: wasteful thoughts and powerful thoughts.

Wasteful thoughts bring heaviness, decrease your enthusiasm and courage, and create doubts in the form of why, what, when, and how – the result of which is depression over small matters. Wasteful thoughts deprive you of achieving attainments. There are many desires, many high hopes, and many plans, but because of lack of will power and determination, the thoughts do not get translated into actions. The pace of thinking is very fast and irrational. Waste thoughts are like a typhoon: They create fluctuation and chaos, deplete your spiritual energy, and waste your time.

Powerful thoughts are focused on only that which you intend to do. The pace of thinking is regular and full of patience. Such thoughts create a sense of inner calm and coolness, which gives a pleasant feeling. Powerful thoughts are benevolent; they enable you to accumulate your spiritual energy and make your time fruitful. The thinking and action are equal, and this balance brings success.

In order for the mind to stay constantly powerful, remember two aspects: Have positive thoughts for the self and positive thoughts for others. When your thoughts are pure and powerful, you are able to transform the negative into positive at the level of thinking. Having positive thoughts for the self is very deeply connected with having positive thoughts for others. If you do not have positive thoughts for the self, you cannot have positive thoughts for others. If you do not have positive thoughts for others, it indicates that you do not have positive thoughts for the self.

You, the soul, use your mind to create both positive and negative thoughts. You must now pay attention because many problems and people are such that you cannot deal with them through words but only with your positive thoughts and vibrations. At present, the majority of souls in the world are influenced by fear and worries. With the power of pure and positive thoughts and good wishes, give the donation of peace.

At this time, there is the need for peace of mind. Through the power of pure thoughts, you are able to have peace of mind and to give others the experience of peace. Along with speaking and acting, are you able to use your mind to send the power of peace to the minds of others? With the power of your mind, are you able to calm and quiet your own senses and heal your own body? When the power of pure thoughts is combined with words, the soul becomes the embodiment of spiritual intoxication, and there is enthusiasm in the actions performed.

Power of the Intellect

The mind creates thoughts as seeds for actions. However, the soul requires a very good intellect to understand, discern, and decide. The intellect works as a mechanism to give sustenance to the seeds of thoughts that are created. Pure thoughts are elevated. When elevated thoughts are sustained, the quality of the intellect is open, clean, and broad and is described as a golden vessel. When wasteful and degraded thoughts are sustained, the quality of the intellect is locked, impure, and narrow and is described as an iron or stone vessel. The intellect is the eye through which there is recognition of the physical and subtle abilities of the soul. The intellect has the ability to discern truth from falsehood and to understand spiritual knowledge from material knowledge. This is why the intellect is also called the voice of conscience.

In between the creation of a thought and the doing of an action, the voice of conscience intervenes: "What is the meaning of this?" "Shall I do it like this or like that?" "Should I do it with that person or the other?" The intellect could sustain the seed of thought by taking water of knowledge and sunshine of power from the Father, which ensures that the seed bears elevated fruit that gives contentment.

Or the intellect could sustain the seed of thought with the support of physical facilities and the energy of human beings, in which case the seed will bear fruit that leads to temporary satisfaction and dependency. It is the intellect that decides which direction to take.

Everything depends on the quality of the intellect. There is value given to the intellect. It is said that when the human intellect becomes insolvent, then one is declared as spiritually bankrupt. The lock of ignorance on some souls' intellects is so strong that they continue to make mistakes in life. Some souls have the strength of concentration to stabilize their intellects instantly, whereas others try so hard but nothing remains in their intellect – it keeps wandering in all directions. Now, at this time, by knowing the quality of the intellect, you act after considering everything and understanding its consequence, so there is no need for regret.

You are now receiving enlightenment. All the spiritual secrets of the whole of humanity are being told to you. The intellect is remembering all the knowledge of what you were and of what you are becoming. It is human beings who have to understand this. Animals will not understand. Knowledge means understanding. A sensible person is someone who achieves success by understanding how to do everything at the right time. The sign of being sensible is that you are never deceived, and the sign of being enlightened is that your intellect is always clean and clear.

Those with a clean and clear intellect would never say of their own actions, "I do not know why I did this." Sensible and enlightened souls can never speak these words, as they would value their every thought, word, and action. The wise intellect is deep and subtle and uses knowledge, powers, and virtues in every action. A stagnant, baby-like intellect is of little use. When the soul is seated on its seat of self-respect, there is love and humility in the intellect. The intellect of the soul should be broad and unlimited and full of love and humility.

Arrogance of the intellect is when there is selfish interest. When your intellect is caught up in any type of confusion, you must realize that you definitely have one or another form of the limited consciousness of "I" and "mine." When there is this consciousness of "I," the intellect spins around in ego and arrogance or being insulted and rejected. When there is the consciousness of "mine," the intellect gets caught up in various forms of attachments to people and possessions. To have the consciousness of "I" and "mine" means there is a lack of self-respect and self-worth. To think "My name will be defamed!" or "I am being insulted!" is called confusion in the intellect. Once the ego becomes involved in this way, then no matter how much you try to put yourself right, you will continue to be confused.

To be free from the limitations of "I" and "mine" is to become a detached observer. To be a detached observer is to clear your intellect. Whether it is anything good or bad, clear it from your intellect by handing it over to the Father: Speak to the Father with honesty and become light. This will keep the discernment power of the intellect clean and clear, and decisions will be timely and accurate.

Power of the *Sanskars*

Sanskars are the latent impressions within the soul that determine the soul's individual and unique form in terms of character, personality, and features. *Sanskars* influence your overall destiny. From the moment you enter the world stage and take a body, your *sanskars* are in a constant process of change.

In your eternal stage, when the soul is in the home up above, the *sanskars* are silent, in a state of deep peace.

When you enter the world stage, in the initial phase of playing your part through your body, you do so in your original stage of being a soul with *sanskars* that are perfect and complete. You are soul conscious, and you experience your true worth and self-respect. Your life at this time is an ongoing dance of harmonizing *sanskars* with others. When your *sanskars* harmonize with the *sanskars* of another, the meeting of love takes place. To harmonize *sanskars* requires a meeting of the hearts and minds. When the laws of the natural world are in harmony with your original *sanskars*, the world stage is a place of peace, happiness, and prosperity.

Then through the process of rebirth, you, the soul, gradually begin to move away from the awareness of your original self and into the awareness of the body. Your actions are influenced by the physical senses and the material world, and as a result the *sanskars* you inculcate are acquired and are no longer original to the soul.

Your awareness of your own identity becomes twofold, and there is duality in your *sanskars*. You are conscious of "I," the soul, and you are also conscious of "my" body. You continue in this state of duality, moving progressively further toward the consciousness of the body until you no longer feel the difference between the soul and the body. This results in *sanskars* of body consciousness: You forget your eternal and original identity and adopt the identity of the body.

Throughout that process, the soul carries good and bad *sanskars* within it. The soul experiences through its body the return of any good and bad actions it has done. No one can say that the soul is immune to the effect of actions. The *sanskars* within the soul are an accurate record of all the soul's actions.

In the body-conscious state, the *sanskars* acquired are molded and shaped by the influence of the five vices of lust, anger, attachment, ego, and greed. When consciousness of the body traps the soul, the *sanskars* accumulated tie the soul in bondage to its body, bodily relations, the material world, and its possessions. But even more subtle, the soul becomes a slave to its subtle servers – the mind, intellect, and *sanskars*. The true reality gets lost, and the physical image becomes the reality that matters. The consciousness of the *atma*, the soul, is replaced by the consciousness of the atom, matter.

Transformation of *Sanskars*

World transformation rests on the transformation of the *sanskars* in the souls of human beings. I have come to teach you in order to liberate you from the jail of the five vices, *ravan*, and to reform your spoiled character. At this moment, your true character has become lost under layers of different identities. The contrast between your original, divine character and your present character is definitely like day and night. To reform your character, you need to transform your *sanskars*.

Child, you now have to make effort to return to your eternal and original *sanskars*, and for this you need to transform your consciousness from being a body to being a soul in a body.

The majority of people know of the accessible potential of the soul. They also know that they are not the embodiment of the full potential of the power of the soul. The full potential emerges from the eternal and original *sanskars* that are intrinsic in the soul. The full potential of the soul is seen through your awareness, your inner stage, and your task.

The power of knowledge awakens within you the elevated awareness of your true identity of being a soul. This awareness of soul consciousness connects you to your original powers and virtues and gives you a sense of your full potential. The deeper you allow yourself to go, the more beautiful the experiences. You experience an inner stage of true worth and self-respect. From this inner stage, your intrinsic elevated *sanskars* emerge and are used in actions for the task of self-transformation. The more the intrinsic *sanskars* are used, the greater the potential for self-transformation and world transformation.

Love, not force, brings about transformation of acquired *sanskars*. You have received knowledge about the soul. However, knowledge has to be inculcated with love, because it is love that attracts you and gives you the power to return to your original *sanskars*. Without love, the power of knowledge would not work. There was none of this in your intellect previously. What was in your intellect before? To transform the self, the intellect turned to worship, chanting, doing penance, and bowing your head. There is a vast difference between the memories of what you were doing and the memories that are being awakened now. You are reminded of this difference of doing something with force and doing it with love. Now that I have reminded you of all this, you should keep it in your intellect and discern for yourself.

The Father is placing you under His canopy of protection and is filling you with love. I know that if there is no love, life seems to be very dry and everything seems difficult. Love is considered such an elevated virtue that people think that love is God. They say, "God is love and love is God." So love is considered as elevated as God Himself! This is remembered because it is Godly love which has given you a spiritual birth, and it is Godly love which becomes the nourishment to nurture the soul and to give it the strength to remove itself from the chains of the vices.

Love has given you the power to experience your true fortune and the lightness to overcome the obstacles that come in your way. So transform your *sanskars* with true, honest love. On the basis of love, difficult things are experienced to be very easy.

It is in relationships that *sanskars* seem the most difficult to transform. When there is harmony of *sanskars*, relationships are sweet and give a lot of happiness. When there is conflict in *sanskars*, relationships are distant and give pain and sorrow. When you fix your heart on relationships with others, your heart breaks into pieces. It is Godly love that brings the pieces of your heart back together into one. Now your heart is fixed on the One who comforts and soothes your feelings. It is My love that makes you great.

Learn how to forget, finish, and merge conflicts of the past and how to bring harmony into the present through giving regard to others. Let there be maturity, mercy, and mastery in your behavior. To harmonize *sanskars* and bring back closeness in interactions, you need the power of love, the power of relationships, the power of cooperation, and the power of tolerance. Be one who has pure and positive thoughts and remove the worries that are accumulated within the self.

All the thoughts you have are food for your intellect. The words you speak are food for your mouth. Your actions are food for your hands and feet. Therefore, you should check everything – your thoughts, words, and actions – for your *sanskars* are connected to all three. What would you call it if you do something first and then think about it afterwards? Therefore, be doubly sensible. Simply make this one aspect your original *sanskar*: First think, and then act. Remember, once the action is performed, a *sanskar* is formed.

Some souls have a *sanskar* of not accepting anything as being insignificant. They would first look at everything and check it carefully before accepting it. So who are you? You are a pure, great soul; you are an elevated soul. Therefore, if you were to accept thoughts without considering them, say something without thinking, or perform actions without discerning, it would not match your greatness.

At the present time of the Confluence Age, you sow the seed of elevated *sanskars*. Without the seeds being sown here, the future tree cannot be created. How will the future fruit emerge if you do not sow a seed at the time when it is the season for planting? The self-sovereigns of the present time will be the world sovereigns of the future. Such self-sovereigns are generous-hearted and are the images of upliftment for everyone.

. . . He stops talking and looks at you quietly. He senses how your mind has expanded to take in all of what He has been telling you, and He brings this lesson to a close. This is enough for now. He will return to give you a third lesson.

As He walks away, you find yourself churning on this study for sovereigns and wondering about this One who has appeared to teach you.

IMPLICATIONS FOR LIFE

To reflect on your eternal identity and your original identity, to know yourself on those terms, and to remain in such thoughts about yourself is said to be thinking of yourself as a spiritual being. This is called the stage of soul consciousness.

THREE

THE SUPREME SOUL ENTERS THE CORPOREAL WORLD

*O*n the day of your third lesson, you are awake very early, before dawn. The moon is finishing its journey across the sky and is breaking through clouds, rimming them in brilliant silver. There are still stars visible in the sky. Your thoughts turn to your previous lesson, and you wonder about your original home, this place where you lived with others like yourself and with your Father, your Mother, in peace.

It is all beginning to look so different now than it did when you first walked through that mysterious door. You are not who you thought you were, and those around you in the world are not who they appear to be. It seems that you are all part of a different, more subtle world, an eternal universe that is somehow dwelling inside of this material world. Who is this One who has appeared as if from nowhere to teach you this study for sovereigns? And why has He appeared at this moment?

Your mind is very quiet as it considers that your eternal destiny might reside mysteriously in a tiny point of light that lives within you. You look at the millions of tiny stars in the sky and imagine the multitude of souls like yourself living together somewhere beyond the sun, the moon, and the stars in a home of light. After a while the first birdsongs break through the silence of the night, and a little while after that, the

horizon begins to lighten. Before the sun crests the horizon, the One who welcomed you here appears in the distance walking towards you. You feel your heart grow warm as you see Him. As He gets closer, you see that He has brought some food for you. He sets it down next to you. He watches you for a few moments and then asks whether you are ready for your next lesson. You thank Him for the food, and as you are spreading out the cloth and preparing to eat the small feast, you encourage Him to continue with today's lesson, hoping He will tell you more about Himself.

He reminds you that this is the auspicious Confluence Age, the most elevated of all of the great ages of humankind. It is an age of great fortune in which those who have been lost for a long, long time acquire divine vision, which allows them to see and recognize things that were invisible to them before. It is as if a third eye has opened revealing the subtle causes and relationships that move the material world. The most important of these subtle relationships, He tells you gently, is the one that He has with you. You stop eating and wait expectantly for what comes next.

He tells you that though He appears to be an old man, this form is not His true form. He, like you, is a soul, a tiny point of light with consciousness. The eternal Being within this body you are seeing is neither male nor female, because in our spiritual essence we have no gender. He tells you that each soul has a unique part to play in the world, and that at this auspicious time, His role requires Him to enter the world and find the very special souls who have become lost and disoriented. He pauses, looking at you and then continues, telling you that He is your eternal, spiritual Father and Mother, and that you are His long-lost child, a spirit, a soul.

For an instant you are startled. Your mind and heart expand to try to embrace this understanding: Your Father as well as your Mother – not just for one life – but for all time! The One you are reunited with here is looking at you with limitless love and understanding. He explains that He knows you completely and has always known you. He has come at this time because He understands what has happened to you and to the world. He also knows about the darkness and vices that have seized the world. "Ravan," he calls them, or "maya", which means illusion.

He has come to awaken you and to uplift you. He tells you not to feel guilty or afraid of mistakes you have made while you were wandering away from Him. The love He has for you is eternal. It never died or even diminished over the long time that you were away.

As the full significance of what He is saying dawns on you, you are filled with lightness and joy. It is as if a heavy burden you were not even aware of gradually lifts, leaving you lighter than air. You feel extremely fortunate – like you are being blessed with a special boon and transported to a new life in which you are surrounded with good omens.

He pulls you close to Him and sits with you in silence to give you a chance to experience the full understanding of what He has said. You realize now the reason for the loneliness you were feeling before. You were an orphan, disconnected from home and family and from the love of your true Mother, your true Father.

He tells you that He is more than your Spiritual Parent. He is also your Teacher whose sole purpose is to awaken within you the divine intellect, which has gone to sleep. Once awakened, this divine intellect has the ability to find the truth, even when it is obscured by maya, *illusion.*

As your Teacher, He has come to tell you the story of the history of the souls and of the world, to help you to rediscover your original qualities and powers, and to tell you what you must do to return home and reclaim your kingdom. He tells you that He will guide you back, but that first you must transform yourself. He will give you a magical agent, a potion, a life-giving nectar, with which to do that. The secret, He says, is "Manmanabhav." As you learn to use this magical agent, your misfortune will vanish and you will be able to claim your rightful inheritance . . .

Teachings

30

called out to Me and said,

"Oh God, my mind has become so peaceless and empty. Come and give me peace of mind." I left My residence of the land beyond sound and came into the land of sound in order to take all My children, the souls, into the state of silence – because in the state of silence there is the experience of immense peace.

You called out to Me, "Come and purify the impure." You call Me the Purifier, the One to remove all the flaws in the souls, who are like diamonds. Therefore, I come and advise you how to become pure and how to radiate the light of your purity.

You called out to the Father, "Oh Bestower of Happiness and Remover of Sorrow, come and make me happy." The Father's plan is to create heaven. I have brought you heaven on the palm of My hand. So the fortune of heaven is now on the palm of your hand.

You called out, "You are the Ocean of Love, and I am thirsty for a drop." You are now merged in the Ocean of Love. You are no longer standing on the shore, thirsty for a drop of God's love.

You called out, "Oh Liberator, Oh Guide, come and take me back home with You." I have come to take you to your sweet home. You will return with Me.

You called out, "Oh, God, the Father, have mercy! Change the angry intellects of human beings so that we do not fight among ourselves." I have come to open your third eye of recognition. I tell you to become soul conscious and follow My elevated directions.

You called out to Me and so I have come. You are the jewels of My eyes, the long-lost and now-found children. I now ask you, "Did we meet before?" *And you say, "You are the same One, and we are the same children who have come to meet You again."*

OUR MEETING

The One who makes the world sparkle like a real diamond, the One who makes matter sparkle like a diamond, the One who makes His children sparkle like precious diamonds, the Father who transforms the old world into a new age, is meeting you.

The gift you receive from the Father at the first moment of meeting is the third eye of recognition. This gift also contains the divine intellect to understand Me and divine vision with which to see Me. On recognizing the Father, the first words that emerge from your lips are "my Father." You are able to recognize the Father with love, pure feelings, understanding, and faith. With this eye of recognition, you are able to know Me, to return to Me, and to belong to Me.

It is only the Father who meets the souls with this clear awareness. As soon as you meet Him, the old awareness – the old recognition which is recorded in the soul as *sanskars* – re-emerges. Then there is the sound of that awareness: "This is the same Father, He is mine." You say, "You are mine," and the Father says, "You are Mine." At the second when the thought of "mine" emerges, in that powerful awareness, in that pure thought, you find a new life and a new world, and you stabilize yourself in the consciousness of "my Father."

The Confluence Age is the time for the meeting of the Father and His children. This sweet meeting is a celebration; it takes place easily. The specialty of this meeting is to attain a spiritual experience – to be lost in the many waves of the Father, who is like the ocean. You surge in the experience of the waves of knowledge, the waves of love, the waves of happiness, the waves of peace, and the waves of power.

KNOW ME AS I AM

My Form

To come close to Me, you have to know Me as I am. Child, I am the Supreme Father, the Supreme Soul, and I am always incorporeal. I do have a form; I cannot remain without a form. It has been explained to you that souls are not visible. In the same way, God is not visible through your physical eyes. A soul cannot be seen; a soul has to be understood. In the same way, the Supreme Soul has to be understood.

Souls are tiny points of light. God is also a tiny point of light, a self-luminous Being. I am also an ocean. I am the Ocean of Knowledge, the Ocean of Peace, the Ocean of Love, and the Ocean of Happiness.

The Supreme Soul is the Seed of the world. I am the Truth, the Living Being, and the Embodiment of Bliss. As the Conscient Seed, I must definitely have all the knowledge, and as the Ever-Pure One, My duty must be the highest of all. I am always called the Supreme Soul. Everyone else is either called a human soul, a righteous soul, or a deity soul.

Child, you, the soul, and I, the Supreme Soul, are both eternal. We are both the same in terms of size and form. Supreme Soul means the one who is constantly pure and viceless. All other souls become pure and impure. The term *human soul* is used. The term *human Supreme Soul* is never used. They use the term *great soul*, but they never say, *Great Supreme Soul*. Supreme means Supreme, the Highest-on-High.

As you progress further, you will come to know Me fully as I am and what I am. You are now still understanding this. What more could you want once you have understood this fully?

My Abode

I come from a faraway land, the supreme abode, which is also called the land of peace. This is My place of residence. It is also the world of light, the *brahm* element. Some people think that the *brahm* element is God. They say that souls merge into the *brahm* element, thinking that it is God in the form of infinite light. Because they do not have accurate knowledge, this is why they say that. In fact, the element of *brahm* is the place where the Supreme Soul resides and where souls reside – as tiny points of light. Just as the sky is an element in the corporeal realm, so *brahm* is an element but in the incorporeal realm. Both are infinite spaces.

People say that God is infinite in size. You understand that God cannot be infinite in size. However, the praise of God is infinite. He is called the Ever-Pure, Unlimited One whose treasure store is never-ending; the Ocean of All Virtues and Powers; the Ocean of Knowledge; the Eternal Truth; and the Almighty Authority. The Father has so many attributes that if you were to turn a whole ocean into ink and all the forests into pens, you could not reach the end of His qualities!

My Image

Sweetest child, I am incorporeal, and in fact, you are also incorporeal, but you take birth and rebirth, whereas I do not. I do not take birth through a womb. I do not become a human being. I do not have a body; all other souls have their own bodies. I always remain bodiless. The One who does not have a body of His own is known as God. Everyone has a physical image. I do not have a physical image. My image is incorporeal.

My Name

Every other soul is only called soul; it is their bodies that are named. I do not have a bodily name; however, the Father's soul is the only soul with a name. So many names are used for Me. Some call Me the Supreme Soul, and some call Me Allah. Some use the word God, and some call Me Jehovah. I am called Ishwar; I am called Alpha. However, in fact, My name is always Shiva. What is the meaning of Shiva? Shiva is the Infinitesimal Point, the Benefactor, and the Seed of the human world tree.

THE FAMILY OF GOD

The first thing I do is bring all of you into the lovely relationship of family. I do not just give you the knowledge that you are souls, but I say that you are My children and I bring you into this lovely relationship of Father and children. After coming into this highest spiritual relationship, a pure relationship of brotherhood is created. Once this relationship is created, what is the result? It turns into the family of God. All members of God's family are seated on the unlimited throne of God's heart. I give you so much regard. I make you sit so honorably on My heart-throne.

The Father sees one desire in the hearts of all the children in the world, and that is the desire for real love. I have come to fulfill that desire. Godly love means selfless love, pure love, and true love. God's love is the basis for life. God's love draws you closer to Him and to each other. God's love frees you from hard labor and makes you experience an easy and constant life. God's love heals the heart and transforms the feelings. God's love brings attainments to all relationships and makes you into a giver. All souls say that they have love for God, but the proof of love for God is to radiate love into the world and let every soul say, "This elevated soul has love not only for the Father, but also has constant love for everyone."

OUR RELATIONSHIPS

The relationship of all souls is first of all with God. You have received the fortune of having the Supreme Soul as your Father, Teacher, *Satguru* (True Guide), and the One who fulfills the responsibility of all relationships. You understand that I am your Father and that I also give you unlimited instructions as the *Satguru*. From the moment you recognize Me as your Father, I also become your Teacher and give you teachings. You receive your inheritance from Me as your Father, and then in the relationship of the *Satguru*, I take you from the old world to the new world. Here, the Father, the Teacher, and the Guide are one and the same!

Father and Child

You are a child and also a master. You are double. To be a child is to have the right to all the Father's inheritance, and to be a master is to have the right to self-sovereignty. From the moment you take spiritual birth, I make you the master of all My treasures – knowledge, powers, and virtues. My treasures are unlimited, and no matter how much is distributed, they are not going to reduce. The Father does not give anyone more or less. Since it is all for the children anyway, why should I give to some more and to others less? Here, whether you are a son or daughter, each of you has the right to receive a spiritual inheritance.

You inculcate the inheritance into your life according to your power and capacity. So remember that you are a master with a right to the Father's inheritance. The treasure store is open and full. Do not just be happy that you become a child. As a child, you have received your inheritance, and if you do not become a master of the inheritance, then what is the purpose of being a child? Do not just be happy with seeing the inheritance, but claim these treasures by claiming the right to self-sovereignty.

I refer to everyone as children because I know that I am the Father of all souls. All the souls of the entire world are My children. I call everyone "child" and say, "sweet children." I call you sweet because you are all My children.

You know that I am your Father. It is not that all souls are the Father. People say that the whole world is a brotherhood. When you are brothers, the Father is proved to be the One from whom you receive an inheritance. If it were a Fatherhood, there would be no question of an inheritance. You have come to claim your unlimited inheritance once again. You do have this faith, do you not?

Mother and Child

I am also your Mother. God, the Mother, is extremely merciful. The unlimited Mother has mercy for all souls. God, the Mother, is a World Benefactor who brings benefit to all and creates hope in souls who have no hope. People serve God, but now God is serving the children. The world server Mother listens to the hope, enthusiasm, and different feelings in the hearts of souls as they share the state of their minds and their circumstances. The children communicate with the Mother through heart-to-heart conversations, through the language of the eyes, feelings, and thoughts. Only the spiritual Mother and the spiritual children understand and experience this means of communication. When the Mother sees the weakness of the child, she feels compassion and gives comfort in the form of support and encouragement to prevent the child from falling into an unconscious state of helplessness and hopelessness. Her constant attention is to transform the weakness into a wonder.

Teacher and Student

Sweet child, your Father has come to teach you. Keep the awareness that you have a Godly student life, and listen to Me as an embodiment of this awareness. Study with happiness and spiritual intoxication.

In other studies, the father is normally separate from the teacher who teaches. However, some children's father is also their teacher, and he teaches them with a lot of interest because of that blood connection and because he knows that the child belongs to him. This Father is also teaching you with so much interest because you belong to Me and because of our eternal spiritual connection. Therefore, you should also study with that much interest. The Father is teaching you directly. I come only once to teach you. I explain everything very clearly.

Child, your Teacher teaches you in a way that no one else can teach. I know you very well, and I make you the most elevated of all. The knowledge of the whole world is in the Teacher's intellect and is now being given to you to understand. I give you the knowledge of the Creator and the beginning, middle, and end of creation. All that I explain is very accurate. Your intellect is becoming broad and unlimited.

Do you have the intoxication that God is teaching you? You are now receiving nourishment for your soul. It is also called the nectar of knowledge. Your intoxication rises when you imbibe it.

You understand that by studying well you become very fortunate. The first fortune is that you become an embodiment of all attainments. You are constantly swinging in the swing of all attainments, whether it is in all virtues, in all the treasures of knowledge, or in all powers. The second fortune is that in every moment, in every breath, and in every thought, you experience the ascending stage in life. Maintain the intoxication that by studying this study, you are becoming elevated. Spend this life learning, laughing, playing, and dancing the dance of knowledge!

The Supreme Teacher is the Bestower of Wisdom. I am the Intellect of the Wise, and I am making you wise. The knowledge I teach makes you into one with a divine intellect and spiritual vision with which to understand and see. What else do the teachings make you? You become the one who can see the three aspects of time and the one who knows the incorporeal world and the corporeal world. Through this study, you also receive the degree of being a master of self-sovereignty.

In this school for souls, you are not being read to from a book of knowledge. Everyone else in the world studies from the various books which have been written. The contrast between this spiritual study and that worldly study is like day and night. The day dawns through the light of spiritual knowledge, and the whole world benefits. There cannot be another teacher like the One who teaches such spiritual knowledge. And there cannot be another university in which the whole universe is being changed. I am your Teacher, and I Myself have no teacher! I have not learned this knowledge anywhere. No one taught Me any of these things. This knowledge is latent within me. I am eternal, and the knowledge latent within Me is eternal.

The Teacher gives you imperishable knowledge. I come and pour the oil of knowledge into the lamps that have almost extinguished. Only when you understand and inculcate My teachings can there be mercy. Child, you have to study with the Teacher and become enlightened. You first have to have this mercy for yourself. Then you can have the enthusiasm to follow the directions. This study is called *Raja Yoga*. It nurtures you and gives you zeal and enthusiasm.

Supreme Guide and Follower

As the Supreme Guide, I give you the great mantra of *Manmanabhav. Manmanabhav* is the mantra that disciplines the mind. It is the mantra for you to conquer the vices and become victorious. *Manmanabhav* means to focus your mind on only One. It is the essence of knowledge and remembrance and is referred to as life-giving nectar. As the Supreme Guide, I give you such a mantra that you become immortal, and your final thoughts lead you to your destination.

Through the practice of *Manmanabhav*, you receive the blessing of all secrets. Every day the Supreme Guide reveals a new secret in the form of a blessing for you to follow. As the *Satguru*, I guide through My *drishti*. *Drishti* is the spiritual vision of the Supreme Soul on the soul, which gives the soul the power to realize itself as a spiritual being and the insight to catch the subtleties of His guidance. This blessing of self-realization received through *drishti* is a permanent blessing, as it makes you the embodiment of remembrance and power, and you are then able to give *drishti* to others.

You have found such a wonderful Guide. It is My duty to show you the destination. This is your true spiritual pilgrimage. You understand that you now have to return to your sweet home of peace. Only the one *Satguru* is the Bestower of Salvation. Only I know the path home.

You are a true follower. You adopt the *Satguru* to take you into salvation. Salvation means peace and happiness. On this pilgrimage, you have to think of where you are going and of your destination. The road of this journey is a little long, and sometimes children become tired and are unable to keep their mind and intellect focused on One.

The *Satguru* is the One who speaks the truth. By following the directions of the *Satguru*, you can easily reach your destination. Sweetest child, the destination is very high, and the ascent is very steep. *Maya* surrounds you like a fog of illusions that clouds your mind. You become lost in such a way that you do not even realize that every step you take is moving you backwards instead of forwards. *Maya* is very powerful. This is why I have become your Guide. Yet, disregard is created in your mind for the *Satguru's* directions, and you begin to follow the dictates of your own selfish desires. Eventually you become unconscious. However, when this happens, the *Satguru* reminds you of *Manmanabhav*, which revives you and makes you conscious again. Therefore, be cautious at every step and remain alert.

You have been calling out, "Oh God, the Father! Guide me!" However, it is wrong to think that I am the Guide of just one. I am the unlimited Guide. I do not only liberate one – I come and grant salvation to everyone. I alone have the task of showing you the path to salvation. The Father needs many helpers. My worthy children become like lighthouses and help the Father show everyone else the path.

Beloved and Lover

The place to accommodate your Beloved is your heart. All souls belong to the one Beloved. The Beloved has now come to make everyone beautiful, to decorate you. This is not a question of anything physical.

The Beloved is pleased to see His lovers who had been lost. You have now been attracted by My spiritual attraction and have come to know and attain your true Beloved. You have reached your true destination. When you come within this line of love, you are freed from all the many different types of laboring because the waves of love and power that you receive constantly refresh you.

You, the soul, are the lover, and you reach out and hold the hand of the Spiritual Beloved. To hold hands and to move forward is the sign of love and cooperation. If while moving along you get tired, the Spiritual Beloved helps you up. I never let go of your hand. As the Spiritual Beloved, I guarantee My hand and company to you, My spiritual lover, for as long as you keep holding on to My hand and staying in My company. The Spiritual Beloved always listens to the songs of the hearts of the lovers. The songs of worries, of labor, of crying out, and of hopelessness are rendered in front of Me, your Beloved, the Comforter of Hearts. In return, I give so much love and understanding that I make the lovers light. Only the Spiritual Beloved and lover recognize the intimacy of faith, loyalty, and trust in this relationship.

Supreme Judge and Self-Sovereign

I am here to make you fearless. I have come to create a kingdom of self-sovereigns. Yours is not a kingdom of fear. I explain the meaning and significance of living your life without fear, repentance, or punishment. I give you understanding through the philosophy of *karma*, through the knowledge of efforts and rewards, and through the consciousness of being an instrument and of being humble. I show you how to accumulate an elevated account and how to incinerate the old accounts through knowledge, *yoga*, and fast efforts. I show you how to judge for yourself at this time and save yourself from repenting for your own ignorance later. With the extra help of love, I give you extra power to transform and save yourself from punishment.

THE ATTAINMENTS OF EACH RELATIONSHIP

To remain absorbed in the love of attainments from each relationship means that no obstacle can make you bow down and become subservient, that is, lose your self-respect. Because of love, you receive help from the Father. You experience constant, immovable, unshakeable, imperishable love and happiness.

By becoming soul conscious, you experience having all relationships with the Father – and you also experience all My powers and virtues. Since God Himself is offering to give you an experience of all relationships, there is no need to go in any other direction. This experience is the most elevated fortune of the Confluence Age. It is called One strength and One support.

THE DIVINE ACTS

It is said, "Dear God, Your divine activities are wonderful!" People realize that there is some power working, and they are thinking about Who that power is. Eventually they will understand the One who is that power. The Father's divine acts transform the world through three powers: the power of truth, the power of purity, and the power of silence.

God's Act of Creation of a New World

The whole world is God's family. The world stage is My place of activity. I am the Creator and Director. As the Creator, I transform the old into new, the impure into pure, and falsehood into truth. I create the new creation within the old creation. There is just the one world, and it changes from new to old.

It would now be said that this is the old world.

It is in the old world that I awaken your consciousness of being a soul and I give you spiritual birth. I give you new birth through a transformation in consciousness. I give the experience of soul consciousness, and everything becomes new. The old identity of body consciousness finishes, and the new life, the new birth, starts.

In a new birth, life is automatically different. The transformation of consciousness means a new life – newness in thoughts, *sanskars*, relationships, and actions. Newness means that I elevate the quality of human beings and the natural elements. Everything becomes new on the basis of the principles and disciplines of My elevated teachings and directions. This is called an elevated birth in an elevated age.

The powerful Creator establishes a link between Himself and each soul. I sow the seeds of making every soul peaceful and happy. Through the elevated study and practice of *Raja Yoga*, souls lend their fingers of cooperation through their own personal transformation, and with faith and determination a new creation is brought into reality.

So why have I come? I have surely come to make the world new. God Himself comes and establishes heaven. I create the new world in order to give My children their inheritance. I carry out such an elevated task with the help of My children. I am the Creator, but you have to understand that I do not create souls. You souls are eternal and imperishable, and the Father too is eternal and imperishable. The Father who creates heaven is the Father who makes souls into the embodiments of purity and peace. You are my creation in that way. You are the creation the Father creates, and so I am also your Mother.

God's Act as Sustainer of Souls and the World

Spiritual love gives you birth – the spiritual birth of God's lap – and now you are receiving spiritual sustenance through blessings from the Father, the Bestower of Blessings. Everyone is receiving sustenance from the same One, at the same time, in the same way. However, the sustenance that has been given is imbibed according to the capacity of each child to receive. Actually, I give elevated sustenance through three relationships of Father, Teacher, and *Satguru*. You receive the inheritance from the Father, and you are sustained by power and virtues. The sustenance received from the Teacher is He decorates you with the jewels of knowledge and makes you wise with His teachings. The sustenance from the *Satguru* is the experience of blessings – when you follow His directions.

You are being sustained by following My elevated directions. I have come to show you the path to happiness. Children receive happiness according to whatever effort each one makes in following the elevated directions.

I show you a very easy method. By becoming a trustee, you automatically become free from attachments and you use everything with cleanliness of intentions. The consciousness of a trustee is that God has given everything to you in trust, and it should be sustained in a worthwhile way. When you consider anything to be entrusted to you, there will be spirituality within, and there will not be any attachment due to the feeling of its belonging to you. You say, "God, everything I have belongs to you." And I reply: "Remain a trustee. God has made you a trustee of your body, mind, wealth, relationships, everything. These are not yours any longer." Would you say they are yours, or would you say you are a trustee? To be a trustee is to use everything in a worthwhile way without the feeling of possessiveness.

The Father sustains all His children with a lot of love. The Father's love and sustenance are received by children who do everything with the awareness of being an instrument with humility. The embodiment of this awareness is the embodiment of power. When you keep in your awareness the elevated fortune that you are a child of God, you naturally feel sustained by Him. When you serve in this awareness, such service is very benevolent – it gives human beings the sustenance of life. This is the greatest and most elevated task.

God's Act of Purifying the World

I come at the Confluence Age. I come just for this short time to purify the world. This is the kingdom of the five vices, *ravan*. The vices are here, and the Purifier Father is also here. The vices make everyone impure. Now that there is no purity, there is no peace or prosperity either. My act of purification is to show you the cause of impurity and to teach you the method to remove these impurities.

The power of purity is not an ordinary power. This power, accumulated over a period of time, is used to give support and strength to the world. When purity is lost, peace and happiness are also lost, and everything becomes divided.

You understand that you accumulate a lot of purity through the power of silence. In silence, there should only be the Father and you. This line of safety is the Godly canopy of protection. When you stay within the line of safety, the force of *ravan* does not have any courage to enter.

The Almighty Father is described as more powerful than a thousand suns. In silence, the soul connects to the Supreme Soul and draws spiritual power. With the power of silence, I give *sakash* lovingly to each of My children. *Sakash* are the rays of spiritual light and might that are transmitted directly from the Supreme Soul to souls. Those children who are in silence are able to catch this current of light and might, and their battery of the soul is recharged. I am your Obedient Servant. My duty is to serve you souls. This is a very subtle service. It is the service of purification. Only you would know whether you accept this service or not.

You now understand that the Father as the Purifier works through the power of silence to bring about transformation. These mountains of stone, that is, the Iron-Aged world, will be changed. Not just all the human beings of the world, but everything – even the five elements – will become *satopradhan*, that is, will return to a state of complete truth and order.

WHAT GOD DOES NOT DO

People say that God is in everything, that everyone is God. They say that I am in the cats and dogs, that I incarnate in fishes and crocodiles. They have put Me into many different species. They say that I am in every speck of dust. Is that My life story? Never mind calling themselves God, they even say that the pebbles and stones are God! They have lost God completely! This is called immense darkness.

People believe there is nothing that God cannot do – that He can even bring the dead back to life. It is not that when someone falls ill, I can cure him or free him from having an operation. No, all souls have to face the consequences of their actions. Although souls are definitely punished for whatever wrong they do, God does not punish souls.

Human beings blame the Father. They say that He is the One who gives happiness and sorrow and yet they still remember God in order to come and grant them peace and happiness. I am the Remover of Sorrow and the Bestower of Happiness, and so how could I hurt anyone? I do not cause violence and sorrow.

There are many natural calamities taking place. These are called "natural calamities," not "Godly calamities." When there are tidal waves of the ocean that destroy everything, why should God be blamed for these? The elements have become *tamopradhan* – in a state of complete disorder. People say that every leaf moves on the orders of God because they think that God is in every leaf. Would God sit and give orders to leaves? Every element of nature has its own laws, and everything moves according to those laws.

There are many who say, "You know everything that is going on inside of us, and we do not need to tell You the secrets of our hearts." It is not that I know the secrets of everyone's heart. Others study for the talent of thought-reading; that does not happen here. I teach you, and I also watch as a Detached Observer. You come here in order to study, and you also can have a heart-to-heart conversation with Me and tell Me what is in your heart.

ALTRUISTIC SERVER

The Father is so innocent. Just see what I take from you and what I give to you in return. I take everything old you have and give you everything new. This is why I am called the Bestower. There is no other Bestower like I am. I am altruistic, and I do altruistic service. I do not have any expectations. I just come to give knowledge to My children, and through My divine acts, I bring about world renewal. I make My children into masters of the world, the land of happiness. I Myself do not become the Master of the World. I serve, but I do not experience the fruits of the service I do. This is called altruistic service, and I am the only Altruistic Server.

... The Teacher's voice comes to a stop, and for a few moments you sit together in silence. The sudden discovery of this hidden Benefactor has transformed everything. Your heart tells you that the things He is telling you are true, and yet ... at the same time, your mind is finding all of this change to be very sudden and is still holding onto the old limited understandings of who you were when you began your search and of the distressed world you were wandering through on the other side of that door. It is as if you have a kind of double vision: In one moment you feel you are the weary seeker who began this journey, and in the next, you are lifted with the clear vision of being a subtle star, an eternal traveler through time, the child of this magnificent spiritual Being who has come to guide and protect you. You can tell that you will need this magic nectar He is talking about so that whenever you feel you are losing your way and being pulled back by the darkness of ravan and the old world, you can call on it, knowing it will sustain you in love and truth.

You want to know more about the story of the souls and the world and about this magical agent He has brought, but He tells you this is enough for today. He will tell you about the history of the world in your next lesson.

41

┌─── IMPLICATIONS FOR LIFE ───┐

Manmanabhav is the mantra that disciplines the mind. *Manmanabhav* means to focus your mind on only One. It is the essence of knowledge and remembrance and is life-giving nectar. *Manmanabhav* is the method to recognize the Father, to belong to Him, and to love Him.

THREE | THE SUPREME SOUL ENTERS THE CORPOREAL WORLD

FOUR

THE DRAMA OF FOUR AGES, THE CYCLE OF TIME

*O*n the morning of your fourth lesson, you awaken to find a large piece of parchment lying on the ground next to your bed and with it a plate of fruit. Your Father has been here and left. Perhaps He has gone for a walk. You take a piece of fruit and lower yourself onto the ground where you open the parchment fully and turn it slightly. It is a large circle that is divided into quadrants. Each quadrant is a different color, and within each there are small images. You lean closer to study the images and are so intent in scrutinizing the parchment that you do not hear your Father approach. Suddenly He is there, and your attention flies from the parchment to Him. He is smiling at you and asks how you slept. You assure Him you slept soundly, though you do not remember when you fell asleep and cannot remember dreaming. You thank Him for the morning gifts, and you point to the parchment, asking Him to tell you more about this picture.*

He nods and settles down next to you, laying the piece of parchment across your laps. His index finger moves across the parchment and comes to rest in the quadrant on the upper right, which is the lightest of the four. It portrays a beautiful land filled with golden light. This, He says, is the beginning of the cycle of time on Earth. Just as a day is a cycle moving from early morning until late at night, and a year is a cycle within which there are seasons, these cycles spin within an even larger cycle, which is of 5,000 years, and within this cycle there are four ages ... plus the auspicious Confluence Age in which we are living now.

Long ago, you fell into kind of a waking sleep, He says, as deep as the one from which you have just awakened. And just as you cannot remember what happened between the time you slipped into sleep and the time you emerged into the morning, likewise you cannot remember when you fell into this millennial sleep or what transpired during that time. But if you could remember the time before you fell asleep, you would remember living in this glorious Golden Age when you had everything you could have possibly wanted – all treasures, all powers, complete sovereignty.

Over the next several hours, He tells you the grandest story you have ever heard. As He is talking, His finger moves steadily around the circle on the parchment. You begin to understand that you, the inner spiritual being, are involved in a sort of play – an epic drama on a scale so vast that you had lost sight of the edges of it. Long ago, when you stepped into your first role in this drama, you knew that it was a play in the physical world and that you, the spiritual actor, were playing a part. In those early times you understood that you were putting on a physical costume, the body, in this limited play, and you would do so easily. Then, when that part was finished, you would set the physical body aside just as easily. But somehow in the series of entries and exits on and off the stage, you had forgotten that it is a play. You had begun to think you were that part, grieving when the part came to an end and clinging to the costume and the role.

Now, it seems that the Director has surprisingly walked onto the stage to talk with the actors, reminding you that you are not these roles. At first you are all disoriented, as if to say, "What is He talking about?" But then, as He continues to explain, you have begun to remember that, yes, before you were on this stage, you were resting somewhere else with Him and with one another in perfect stillness and peace. The experience of being in this drama has somehow swept you away, and in the pageantry and excitement of it all, the memory of your home has slowly faded until finally, you thought this stage was your home and this costume was you.

He explains that this play, unlike all other dramas, is self-renewing, and that now those who will begin the first act of the new drama must begin to prepare. The first act of the drama opens in a Golden Age, a time of extreme purity. It is the time that is sometimes referred to as paradise, and those who are fortunate enough to live in this time are very, very happy. The second act of the drama also takes place in a pure time

— not as pure as the first act — but still very pure and beautiful. It is known as the Silver Age, and those who have parts in this age are also very happy. The world stage then undergoes a kind of transition and moves to a third act, the Copper Age. Those who live in the Copper Age have forgotten that they are spirits and believe that they are bodies, the costumes they have taken on. This is the age of commerce, bargaining, and trading — a time of merchants and also soldiers. Those who live in the Copper Age begin to experience sadness, anger, and limitation. It is the time when ravan, *the vices, first enters the world. Then follows the Iron Age, a time of extreme darkness and conflict. This, He reminds you, is where you were when He found you and led you through that magical door and into the final age, the short and very auspicious Confluence Age.*

As He explains, you again experience a kind of double vision. It feels as if the part you have played is real and at the same time that what He is saying is also real. You feel as if you are both the eternal spiritual actor playing temporary physical roles, and that you are also this physical role . . .

Teachings

46

Father comes at this time to tell you things of knowledge. He explains that His teachings tell the story of the world. What is the story? It is of souls being wealthy in the early morning and becoming beggars by the evening. When you are wealthy, you do not hear this story. It is at the Confluence Age that you hear the story of the world history and geography and of how you can change from a beggar to a prince.

The Father is telling you the story of the past. It is a very short story. It is told to you in a nutshell! This story is of four ages, plus a fifth one which is the leap age, the Confluence Age. It is the story of the cycle of time in which the world moves from day to night and then from night to day. In between the night and the day, there is the dawn. It is also the story of a variety play of all souls — the drama of actors on the world stage, making their entrances at different times and playing their variety roles.

The Father has come to awaken the fortune of human beings. The Father looks at the children and thinks: You have been wandering around on the path of search. You practiced devotion for so many births. What was it all for? In order to find God and to reclaim your lost sovereignty. Now it is the end of your searching. God is now giving you the fruit of that search.

THE CYCLE OF TIME

This world cycle turns, second by second. There is no end to it. Minute by minute, the ticking continues as the world cycle continues to move. One second cannot be the same as the next. This world cycle makes one complete turn every 5,000 years. The world is eternal; it can never be destroyed.

The world drama, too, is eternal. You are actors in this drama, and you have your part recorded within you. Not a single soul can be excused from playing a part in this eternal drama. Everyone has to play a part. Your part continues eternally. It can never end, even though one second cannot be the same as the next. There is such subtlety in understanding this. There is only this one drama, and there is only one world where this drama is played. You understand that you are all actors and that you come at your accurate time onto the world stage to play your part. Every soul enters the world in its original stage, numberwise, at its accurate time.

I explain the secrets to you. On listening to the secrets, you should not ask when the cycle was created. It is eternally made. If I had created it, you could then ask Me when I created it. This world cycle is eternal. So the question of when or why it began cannot arise. If you were told that it began at such-and-such a time, you would then ask, "When will it end?" But it never does! This world cycle continues to spin.

It has four quadrants. It is divided accurately into four quarters — golden, silver, copper, and iron. None is slightly more or less. Then there is a fifth, incognito, short age, which no one knows about, and this is called the auspicious time of the confluence of the two cycles.

THE WORLD STAGE: THE BEGINNING

This world is a huge stage on which this unlimited play is performed. It has huge lights — the sun, moon, and stars — which are constantly lit. In the beginning, the elements of matter are in perfect order and work as instruments of happiness. The land and all its treasures are first class. The entire planet and ocean are without partitions and divisions. Everything is *satopradhan* and operates on the principle of truth.

The world and matter are completely pure, and there is natural beauty. The vegetation with its greenery, with the movement of its leaves, plays various forms of beautiful music. The swaying of the leaves of the trees and their movement make different varieties of natural rhythms. The birdsongs fill the air with natural melodies.

The water flows through natural herbs and acquires special properties such that it always remains pure. The sun's rays do the work of different forms of light and energy. Everything is natural. The weather is always like springtime, and all the elements remain in order. There is plenty of land, and it does not cost anything. People can take as much land as they want, and there is no municipal tax. Matter serves everyone, and everything is plentiful.

The pure earth gives in abundance. The water of the ocean is like milk, and the sky is like a canopy of protection. The ones who rule are benevolent bestowers. The character of all the people is divine, and their religion is peace and nonviolence. The kingdom is operated by refined atomic energy.

The mines are full of precious diamonds and other valuable stones which are used to decorate the buildings. The buildings are like palaces.

Nothing remains unattained. The world stage is in perfect order. It is called the land of truth, the land of happiness and peace, and the land of immortality. This is the state of the world stage in the Golden and Silver Ages, the first half of the cycle of time – the day of the human world.

Morning: The Golden Age

The cycle of time begins with the Golden Age. The Golden Age is called *Satyug*. *Satyug* means the age of truth. It is also called the land of happiness, heaven, paradise, and the Garden of Allah. As well as happiness, there are also purity and peace there. This is why a lion and lamb have been shown drinking water from the same pool. At that time, the world is *satopradhan* – in its highest state of truth and purity. The five elements of matter are the instruments of happiness. Matter is in a state of complete purity with the highest degree of order, and only truth prevails.

Souls arrive onto the world stage in the Golden Age with their awakened fortune. Souls come from the home with a lot of spiritual power. This power is a result of their remembrance of God at the Confluence Age, which gradually filled them to capacity and made them soul conscious. This accumulation of power from God brought them back to their original power of complete soul consciousness. Their intrinsic, elevated *sanskars* are the rewards of the study of knowledge and the inculcation of divine virtues and spiritual powers. These treasures are innate in the souls as their Godly inheritance. They enter the world in their highest living form.

When they first come down from the home into the elevated world, they are *satopradhan*. Incorporeal, *satopradhan* souls enter corporeal *satopradhan* bodies. They live by the laws of soul consciousness in harmony with the natural laws of nature. They are the souls who live by the highest codes of conduct.

Their *sanskars* are completely viceless, and their sense organs are absolutely nonviolent. Their personalities are pure and divine. They are complete with all divine virtues and all celestial arts and talents. This is the original state of divinity of souls who come onto the world stage as human beings when the world is in its *satopradhan* stage. Because of their high stage of purity and divinity, they came to be called divine beings, or deities.

The soul leads a full life in the land of immortality, the Golden Age. The pure soul enters a body made of the *satopradhan* elements, and both the soul and the body are pure. The beauty is natural. The soul is ever-healthy and ever-wealthy, and the life span is long. Birth involves no pain at all, and there is no such thing as untimely death. With great happiness, at the right time, the soul leaves one body and enters the womb of its next mother, and fortune continues to sparkle on the center of the forehead.

In the land of truth there is no form of falsehood. Their language is one of love. These beings whom we now call deities have a great deal of love for one another. Their way of interacting is with pure thoughts and pure feelings, and there is deep recognition through the eyes. Love and light are clearly visible in the eyes. They speak softly, sweetly, and use few words.

All hearts are full, so they do not have to make any effort there to attain anything. There are no desires, and nothing is lacking. This is paradise, where souls remain constantly happy, where everyone gives happiness. The deities have constant, imperishable happiness.

The self-sovereign deities have a double crown – one is the crown of light, which represents their high level of purity, and the other is the crown of jewels, which represents their ruling power. They are completely enlightened and wise rulers.

The crown of light means that as *satopradhan* self-sovereigns, their *sanskars* are full of the elevated, unifying principles of life, called *dharma*. These elevated principles are the basis of their elevated actions. Deities do not worship anyone. They do not remember God. Their religion is the highest one of nonviolence.

They do not need fortresses, etc. A fortress is built for safety. There are no fortresses in the kingdom of the deities. No one is there to make war. This is called the time of peace, purity, and prosperity in the world.

Paradise definitely exists. It is the time when the world and its human beings are the holiest and the highest. However, just as when a building is built and at the beginning it is new, and then after some years it begins to show signs of wear and tear, in the same way, after playing their role for the full span of the Golden Age, there is a slight decrease in the degrees of purity and perfection for both the deities and the world. The degrees of purity within the soul diminish little by little with each rebirth. Degrees of purity in matter decrease as well.

Afternoon: The Silver Age

Then the world cycle enters its second quarter, which is called the Silver Age. The Silver Age is called *Tretayug*. Even though it is still the land of happiness, it is called semi-heaven because the alloy of silver has been mixed into matter, which had been golden in its quality. There is a high degree of order, but it is not the highest, and the light of truth also reduces a little.

Even though the Golden Age changes into the Silver Age, everything continues to function within the same divine system. The residents of the Silver Age have their own duties, and the exchanges and dealings are conducted with great love and respect.

The Silver Age is semi-heaven, but it is still the land of happiness and it is still very entertaining. Residents of the Silver Age have no burdens. Everyone young and old has wisdom. They are artists, painters, and musicians. The method of learning is through music, poetry, and the arts. Learning is according to innate wisdom, talents, and arts and does not require expertise. Playing musical instruments is natural. As soon as the fingers touch the instruments, music is naturally played.

From the beginning of the Golden Age to the end of the Silver Age, souls live for half a cycle as self-sovereigns. Then, by taking rebirth, they definitely climb down the ladder, and the intellect begins to weaken. Whatever power they have accumulated by connecting their intellect in *yoga* to the Father at the Confluence Age now finishes. By the end of the Silver Age, the intellect begins to stumble in search of its lost sovereignty. The Silver Age completes, and the act changes.

Evening: The Copper Age

The third quarter of the world cycle is the Copper Age. The Copper Age is called *Dwapuryug*, which means the age of duality. The world is no longer called heaven or semi-heaven as it enters into an era in which happiness is mixed with sorrow. It is called the land of semi-sorrow. The world is *rajopradhan*, which is a middling stage of purity. That is, purity is mixed with impurity, order with disorder, and truth with falsehood.

The Father explains that as souls take rebirth, their purity diminishes and they gradually begin to change from pure to impure. In the *rajopradhan* stage, the intellect begins to seek fulfillment through the sense organs, and the soul develops the *sanskars* of mixing everything. There is the mixture of soul consciousness and body consciousness. The soul-conscious "I" of self-respect is mixed with the body-conscious "I" of arrogance, and there is the experience of happiness and sorrow. Attachment is mixed into pure love of family life, and relationships begin to give sorrow. Limited selfish desires are mixed with the natural benevolence and sense of abundance of the earlier ages.

It is because there is mixture that there is heaviness, just as pure gold becomes heavy when alloy is added. In the same way, when selfish desires are mixed with elevated directions, there is heaviness in the soul. The mind and intellect develop the habit of acting on selfish desires. Such selfish desires are controlled by illusion, ignorance, and the vices, and they weaken the power of stability and concentration of the mind and intellect. The soul steps down from its self-respect, and its reins of power are handed over to the senses and sense organs of body consciousness.

You understand that to begin with, when the soul is pure, the actions – *karma* – and unified spiritual principles – *dharma* – are elevated. Even though actions are performed through the sense organs, there is freedom within action, which results in happiness and harmony. When purity is lost, the souls experience a void, an emptiness. However, it is when the souls become trapped in their sense organs for attainments that these actions tie the soul in bondage and they become corrupt. The *karma* and the *dharma* are separated, and the *karma* is now connected to illusion and ignorance. When the actions are no longer aligned with the elevated spiritual principles, there is an effect left for every action performed. Whatever right or wrong actions performed are accounted for, and the result of that right or wrong action is definitely received in the next birth. This is the Law of Cause and Effect that begins from the Copper Age.

Sages and holy men say that the soul is immune to the effects of action. However, it is the soul that has to take rebirth according to its actions, and so it cannot be immune. It is the soul that performs good and bad actions. In the Copper Age, actions become sinful because of the influence of body consciousness, and *sanskars* are acquired accordingly.

The systems begin to change in a visible way. At the beginning of the Copper Age, the power and authority of the rulers are still great, but as time passes, both of these are gradually misused.

The Father is explaining to you how the new world becomes old. Day by day, the souls continue to decline as they become trapped in the forgetfulness of body consciousness and eventually fall onto the path of sin. After falling onto the path of sin, their life span also reduces.

Spiritual happiness vanishes, and the religious founders come to establish religions and to support souls through their messages. However, souls continue to search and call out: "Oh God, the Father! Give us blind ones sight so that we can recognize our Father." They stumble and call out to the Father for the third eye of recognition with which to receive salvation and to meet Him.

In their search there are many partitions created, and other lands come into existence. The name and features change in different ways during the many births now on different lands. Some souls take more births than others, but all souls experience peace, purity, and happiness as their birthright when they first descend onto the world stage.

In the Copper Age, the soul's quality of reasoning is based on an understanding of bargaining: "If I do this, then I will get that in return." "Oh God, if you do that for me, then I will give You this in return." This bargaining intellect leads to a stronger consciousness of the ego and arrogance of "I" and of the attachment and possessiveness of "mine" – and to a further descent for the soul.

While saying "today and tomorrow," the Golden, Silver, and Copper Ages pass, and the souls continue to become degraded from elevated. There are not as many sins at the start of the Copper Age as there are later on. Being influenced by the vices, souls are trapped and led down the path of sorrow. Human beings continue to follow the path of sorrow. Those who were once the bestowers of happiness have now become bestowers of pain and sorrow. This world, which was once heaven, has now become hell. Souls wound one another with the swords of lust, anger, attachment, ego, and greed. The five vices become such big enemies! The souls come face to face with sorrow.

Night: The Iron Age

The last quarter of the cycle is the Iron Age, which is also known as *Kaliyug. Kaliyug* is the age of total darkness and insolvency. Happiness vanishes and is replaced by sorrow. This age is remembered by many different names: the sinful world, hell, and the homeland of sorrow. In its *tamopradhan*, most degraded stage, the land is barren and old. The world reaches to its state of absolute impurity, all truth is lost, and there is only chaos.

Elements of matter – air, water, earth, fire, and sky/ether – have gone through their golden, silver, copper, and iron stages according to their own natural laws and have reached their lowest stage.

The stage of the whole world is in descent. There is peacelessness and sorrow throughout the whole world. People are crying out for peace and happiness. However, it is impossible for anyone to remain constantly peaceful in this age where there is only sorrow. The Copper Age is the land of semi-sorrow, but the Iron Age is called the land of total sorrow.

Souls are in their *tamopradhan* stage. This stage is of complete unrighteousness and falsehood. The quality of the *sanskars* is of impurity, and there is very little light and power left in the soul. Truth is totally forgotten and the voice of conscience is asleep. The intellect is stumbling in total darkness of ignorance. The mind is like a wild horse running at a fast speed, and the heart is broken into a thousand pieces seeking fulfillment in relationships.

The search for God and the truth has extended to all corners of the world. People are praying a great deal and enduring sorrow at the same time. Surrounded by the vices, even though they study matters of devotion, they continue to fall further down. People continue to worship without understanding anything. They continue to build temples to the deities without knowing their biographies. All of this is called blind faith. They worship and call out for liberation from sorrow and salvation from the world of sorrow.

Relationships are *tamopradhan* and give a lot of sorrow. There have never been so many relationships as there are at this time in the Iron Age. There is conflict and violence at all levels of life. The value for human life is at its lowest.

There is no power and authority left in the rulers. It has become the rule of people by the people, leaders are sitting on seats of uncertainty, and there is very little respect.

Having spent all of their wealth, people have become poverty-stricken, and they call out, "Oh God! Oh Father! Liberate us from sorrow. Take us to our abode of peace and happiness." By wandering around for half a cycle, you wore yourself out and lost hope. Because of being ignorant as to who you really are, you picked up so much sorrow in the land of sorrow.

The soul was 100 percent solvent, and like the degrees of the moon, its light has decreased until there is a very faint line left. It takes one month for the moon to decrease from its complete stage, that is, from being full. Ultimately just a line is left. The moon does not become nonexistent. The same happens to souls; but for the soul, it is a question of the whole cycle. Its light, too, is never completely extinguished. In the same way, the purity of matter has decreased, and this is causing upheaval in the form of natural calamities.

THE WORLD STAGE: THE END

Now the world has become completely impure and old. Why are the terms "the land of sorrow" and "the land of happiness" used? Everything depends on purity and impurity.

People use the names heaven and hell. The world in its present state cannot be called heaven. It is those with a stone intellect who believe that because they have wealth and palaces, etc., that this is heaven. However, you know that heaven is in the new world. People at this time are very unhappy. The soul experiences so much pain through the different diseases of the body in this land of sorrow. In the land of happiness, there is no bodily disease or pain. Here the hospitals are full.

In the pure world there is only one kingdom, whereas in the impure world there are many kingdoms. Here, the population continues to grow, the earth is barren, and the seeds that are planted have no strength left in them. At present, this earth is like a graveyard. So many bombs and missiles are being made; they are not being made simply to be stored. They are refining them more and more and are testing them from time to time. Rehearsals of war continue to take place, and then it will be the finale.

At the end, the splendor that science has produced is so great that its inventions are compared to the Golden Age. It has also produced such materials that people understand that destruction is also taking place. They say they are making preparations for peace as they manufacture more bombs. As the possibility of destruction comes closer, people are searching for God. They understand that if destruction takes place, there must definitely be someone who is carrying out creation as well.

Mountains of sorrow have now fallen, and they will continue to fall. There has to be a limit to the *tamopradhan* stage. This old world now has to change. This Earth once again has to change from *tamopradhan* to *satopradhan*. There is now a short time left. This Earth is again about to change from the Iron-Aged world to the Golden-Aged world.

Child, the old world is now coming to an end. Nearly all the actors have appeared; only a few souls still have to come. When a play ends, all the actors come onto the stage. It is at this time that all the actors are present; nothing can be changed in this. The Creator, the Director, and the actors all stand together. Child, you can understand that this drama is now about to reach its conclusion. All souls have to come down here to play their part. The population continues to grow.

DAWN: THE CONFLUENCE AGE

The Confluence Age is the ending of the night and the beginning of the day. The Father comes at this auspicious Confluence Age to give knowledge and to tell you the story of immortality. He gives you the third eye of recognition with which to understand and experience. The day dawns through the light of knowledge.

The Father changes night into day through knowledge. The Father comes to awaken the fortune of human beings.

This leap age lasts only for a short time. The Father is the Benevolent One. Only He can tell you why there has been such a loss in the world. No one knows who makes the world *tamopradhan* and who then makes it *satopradhan* or how the world cycle spins.

Now be soul conscious, continue to remember the Father, and spin the cycle of self-realization. Think about the rise and fall of the world.

Only the one Father comes and liberates everyone and grants salvation to those of all religions. He says: I have now come to take you back to your home. I have become restless without you. As the time is approaching, I become restless. I feel that I must go to the physical world. The children are very unhappy and are calling out for Me to come. I feel deep compassion for them. I feel that I must go to them. As the time approaches according to the accurate moment in the drama, the thought arises in Me that I have to go.

The Father explains your part from the beginning through the middle to the end. In the beginning I made you children so wealthy. You were given so much prosperity. The world was so elevated and prosperous. So what did you do with it all? I am asking you: Where is all the wealth I gave you? Where has your fortune of the kingdom of self-sovereignty gone? I made you into the masters of the world. What did you do to your sovereignty? You were the masters of the whole world! The earth and sky and all the elements served you!

All souls are children of the one Father. The Father now asks His sweet child: Do you understand what the Father is saying? You have now ended up in the foreign kingdom ruled by the vices. Your enemy is the vices, not one another. You lost the fortune of your own kingdom of self-sovereignty to the vices. Remember the history of your victory and defeat. Do not forget this! Souls say that there should be peace in the world. It is because this world is now *tamopradhan* that there is peacelessness. This is a play about peace and peacelessness; it is a play about happiness and sorrow.

It is only once in the cycle that you receive your inheritance of love, peace, purity, happiness, and powers directly from the Father, and it then becomes eternal. This is why this drama is a play about remembering and forgetting. I come and remind you of your original and eternal self, and through this you re-claim your lost kingdom. I am making you beautiful once again and will then receive you in the abode of peace, your sweet home. You truly do receive your inheritance from the Father. Understand who you are and who you belong to. Why do you consider yourself anything less?

I come and give you real knowledge. Only the Father can give you this spiritual knowledge. The Father says: Now become soul conscious. Remember Me, your Supreme Father, the Supreme Soul. Only through remembrance will you become *satopradhan* once again. The Father is now creating heaven once again. The Father only comes once in the cycle to teach you *Raja Yoga* and to re-create the land of immortality. He is changing the jungle of thorns into a garden of flowers. He is teaching you how to become the bestowers of happiness once again.

You must now once again claim the fortune of your kingdom of peace and happiness. All the *sanskars* of your future lives begin now from this present life. The disc of the soul never wears out because the soul is imperishable, and the part recorded within it is eternal. All the billions of souls have an eternal part. It is like a record that is played continuously. No two souls can have the same part.

Only at this time do you receive knowledge from the Father. You are being uplifted with knowledge. This is the time that you are called an effort-maker. You listen and imbibe the teachings, and on the basis of this understanding you follow the Father's directions. Your greatness is seen in the quality of your efforts. Effort at this time is given greater importance. Do not just sit back and wait for your reward to come to you. A reward cannot be received without making effort. Your greatest effort is to remember who you are and your self-sovereignty. Your greatest fortune is that the Father is giving you directly the most elevated knowledge and is sustaining you with love.

Those in the Golden and Silver Ages do not have this knowledge. There, they are soul conscious but not God conscious. Those in the Copper and Iron Ages do not know this knowledge either. They are body conscious and are searching. It is when you enter the Confluence Age that you receive this knowledge. As you study this knowledge, you are reminded of everything. You remember who you are and who your Father is. You remember the history of your victory and defeat. You are once again becoming the master of the land of peace and happiness.

. . . It seems that you have almost stopped breathing and have become spellbound as your Teacher has carefully laid out this story of your long journey through time. This, you realize, is what He was referring to when He talked about your journey into forgetting. You fix your attention back on Him, listening carefully . . .

Going Home

It has been a long time since you left your home. You have forgotten the way to return there, and so the Father has come to show you the way. You have been inviting the Father to come, saying, "Take us home! Take us to the land of peace!" Now the Father says, "Oh souls! Ask your heart how you can return home impure." Now that you have to return home, you definitely have to become pure. You also understand that you are now given the secret method to become pure. This is the method I give you cycle after cycle. Consider yourself to be a soul and remember Me, the Supreme Soul. This is *Manmanabhav!* This is the fire of remembrance through which your sins will be burned.

That is your sweet home of silence. You now have to return home, and then from there you have to go down into your kingdom. Ultimately, these are the two things you have to do: you have to return, and then you have to come down again. Some have a long rest in the land of peace. Some do not rest there for long; they have an all-round part.

Not everyone will return to the world stage at the same time. Those who do not have a part at the beginning will remain in the land of peace. You know that each human being of the whole world has a part to play in the world drama. The actors must be sitting somewhere while waiting to come and play their part. Souls come down from up above and play their parts at the accurate time in the drama. Souls do not return to the home in between the ages. Souls take rebirth from their first birth in the drama until they reach the end of the cycle.

Souls cannot be liberated from playing their part in this drama. They cannot attain eternal liberation. They cannot stay forever in the home. People go to so much trouble searching for peace. They do not understand that they were in the abode of peace, their home, and that they came down here to play their role.

Every soul plays its own individual role, and then, when all souls return home, each soul goes to its own particular place. Each soul has to return to its own place, in its own section, and then has to come down again to play its part. Each one's role is now ending, and all souls are to return to where they came from. Everyone comes from the abode of peace, and all souls have to return to their home.

All souls return home at the same time. You have to return home on time. It is not that you can go faster and reach there earlier, no. It is not in your hands to go sooner. This is fixed in the drama. Just as there is praise for the Father and the souls, there is also praise for the drama!

THE CYCLE CONTINUES . . .

The world is eternal; it can never be destroyed. People say that annihilation takes place. However, this does not happen. It is against the law of nature for complete annihilation to take place. Why is this? Because all souls' parts are eternal and cannot be destroyed. This is a spiritual secret!

This is a cycle of coming and going within the drama. Each soul has its own complete role contained within it. It is as though the shooting of the film starts from the beginning. However, this shooting really takes place eternally. This history and geography of the world continue to repeat. Minute by minute the ticking continues. The whole reel repeats. It unwinds and is rewound, and then the same thing repeats again. This huge reel is so wonderful! It cannot be measured. Everyone's role ticks away. One second cannot be the same as the next. This cycle continues to turn.

. . . As the Father finishes, His finger is resting at the top of the circle, at what would be the 12 if this circle were a clock, and your head feels full as if for the past few hours you have been a spectator in a vast play with a cast of millions . . . or billions. You can see that on the left side of His finger is the tiny Confluence Age, before that the dark Iron Age, and on the right the luminous Golden Age. This clearly is a time of great significance. He sees you are lost in thought, and after a couple of minutes, He stands up to go, inviting you to ponder in silence what He has been telling you. He reminds you again about the magical nectar He has given you, "Manmanabhav." When you use it, this will help you to remember Him and what He has told you, to remember your true home, and to look ahead to the splendid world of light awaiting you when you walk onto the stage again.

IMPLICATIONS for LIFE

It has now entered your intellect that you were
elevated and that you can once again become
like that. Spin the cycle of self-realization
with the gifts of your divine intellect and
spiritual vision. This means to realize
the cycle of your many births in the Golden,
Silver, Copper, and Iron Ages and to let
your memories return.

FIVE

THE LIVING CREATION AS
THE HUMAN WORLD TREE

*A*s your next lesson begins, your Teacher finds you in a garden, sitting beneath a huge tree with long branches stretching out in all directions. This particular tree is a banyan tree. Its branches are vast and have sent down their own stringy roots into the ground; but the original trunk of the tree has decayed, disappearing many years ago.

He greets you warmly and is delighted to find you beneath this tree, because the lesson He wants to explain to you next is actually about a tree of sorts.

He sits on the ground across from you and motions towards the tree. At this time, the human world is like this vast banyan tree beneath which you are sitting. Its branches are alive, but the original roots and trunk of the tree are gone; they disappeared thousands of years ago. Now, a new human world tree must be planted, because there is never a time when there are not human beings on the Earth.

He tells you that He is the Seed of this new tree. Just as the seed of a physical tree holds the knowledge of the trunk, the branches, and the leaves, He holds the mysterious knowledge about the trunk, the branches, and the leaves of the very diverse human world family tree. This is the time when the new tree is planted. As you study this knowledge with Him, you are learning what you must do to help in the creation of this new human world.

You are listening intently, but you are not sure you understand what He is saying. He continues: At the time when the trunk is growing, the human family is small and unified, and the very atmosphere is infused with peace, purity, and happiness. It is as if everyone belongs to one large family or clan. Centuries later, when people tell stories about that time, they refer to the people in that time as the deity clan and to the place as paradise or Eden. The deity clan expands very slowly for more than two thousand years.

After a time, He says, the tree begins to branch out in several directions, and the atmosphere and activity of the human world family changes. People begin to leave the land where they have been peacefully co-existing. They become merchants and traders in spices and silks, and they begin to form armies. Special souls arrive to found new religions, and as they do, new branches appear on the human world tree. The founders of main branches are those whose names and stories are renowned throughout the world: Abraham, Buddha, Christ, and Mohammed. There are many others who are less well known who also begin new branches of the tree.

As each of these special religious founders comes to Earth from the soul world, the many souls who belong to the new religious families follow these founders into the world. Those who come in these new religious families are fresh and pure, untouched by the darkness and illusion that have entered the world. They bring new hope and wisdom into the world. And so the branches grow and the tree expands and diversifies until it is alive with a variety of languages, beliefs, cultures, and ways of understanding.

As the centuries pass, the branches continue to grow, and those who were new and fresh become degraded and confused. Finally the tree is groaning under the immense weight of these many branches, and the world is made heavy with the vestiges of ravan – greed for material things, lust for people and property, and wars – many of them lasting for generations. The natural world is spent, exhausted from being overused and exploited. Eventually the tree is so old and weak that it is vulnerable to the forces of nature. At that time, a new tree must be planted. And that time, He says, is this time . . .

Teachings

I come as the Seed of the tree of the human family at the auspicious Confluence Age. I come from the incorporeal world and remind you that originally all souls reside in the land of peace as God's family. In the incorporeal world, the home of the souls, there is the tree of souls. In that tree of incorporeal souls, each soul has its own place. Souls come from the home and enter bodies to play their parts on the field of action. No one can see how a soul enters or leaves a body. However, what can be seen is how souls play their parts and how the tree of the human family grows.

THE SEED OF THE TREE

The Father is the Seed of the human world tree. My praise is sung as the Truth, the Conscient Being, and the Embodiment of Bliss. The knowledge of the whole tree, which is now being given to you to understand, is latent within Me. I am such a tiny point, yet the full knowledge of the tree is contained within Me, the Ocean of Knowledge.

This tree is a living tree of souls, and it has only one Seed. Souls cannot be called the Seed of this tree. Only the Supreme Soul is called the Seed of the human world tree. There are no fruits such as mangoes growing on this tree. The seed of a tree that gives fruit is beneath it in the earth, and the tree grows from that seed. If the seed of a mango were conscient, it would explain that it is the seed and that this is the way the tree emerges from it. However, that seed is not conscient.

There is only one human world tree, and its Seed is conscient. The Seed of this tree is up above. In this living tree, the Seed, the Father, is above, and the tree of humanity is below. The human world tree is like an inverted tree. The Father is the Seed. Human beings cannot call themselves the Seed. The Seed would surely have something new, something that no one else has. The Seed definitely has the full knowledge of the beginning, middle, and end of the tree!

The Father, the Seed, now explains the human world tree to you. This explanation is very essential. No one knows how the creation and sustenance of this tree takes place. I have all the knowledge of the creation, the sustenance, and the decay of the whole tree. Ask anyone, "How does the world tree emerge? How is it sustained? How long is its life span? How does it grow, and how does it decay?" No one would be able to explain any of these things. Now that you belong to the Seed, you are able to understand the tree.

This whole tree is God's tree. The main thing is that all souls are brothers. The Father of all souls is the One whom everyone remembers. The new tree is created through Him. Imbibe the knowledge of the Seed and the tree in your intellect.

The Family of Humanity as a Human World Tree

This is the tree of the family of humanity. You are the family of God. In the sweet home, you are an incorporeal family of souls, the children of the Supreme Father, the Supreme Soul, and then you become the physical family of human beings. This is the most wonderful family. There is no question or doubt in this. All are the eternal children of the One Father.

The human world tree is the living creation. It is the genealogical tree of the human family. This is a variety human tree, as it accommodates the unique part of every soul. This is a huge, unlimited tree. The leaves of the tree are countless; no one is able to count them. The number of human beings continues to increase by hundreds of thousands. The Father explains everything very clearly; there is no question of blind faith in this.

Just as the world cycle has four parts, the tree of the family of humanity also has four parts. The trunk of the tree is the Golden and Silver Ages, and the branches are the Copper and Iron Ages. The tree grows slowly. The trunk, branches, twigs, and new leaves of the tree continue to emerge as souls continue to come down from the soul world to play their parts. Everything has four parts. All souls too go through the golden, silver, copper, and iron stages of life. Through birth and rebirth, the soul goes through the different stages. It is the soul that becomes golden, silver, copper, and iron. Alloy is mixed in the *sanskars* of the soul.

This tree is also called the tree of the variety religions. The deity dynasty is the trunk, and then other branches of the world's religions emerge from that. Just as you have a bouquet of flowers, this world tree is like a bouquet of flowers. The Original Eternal Deity Religion is at the center of the bouquet. Then the main religions emerge, and then all the expansion takes place from that. Each branch represents one of the world's religions, and each has to go through its own golden, silver, copper, and iron stages. These are the four stages that the entire world tree goes through.

New souls are pure, and so there is praise of such souls when they first come onto the field of action and take their place in the human world tree. Every soul first receives happiness and praise. Every soul brings its own specialty and adds its unique sparkle to the human family tree.

By belonging to the Seed of the tree, there is a connection with all the souls of the entire tree. You belong to the unlimited family of the human world tree. How the new tree emerges is incognito. The Father comes in an incognito way and also gives you this knowledge in an incognito way. You know that the sapling of a new tree is now being planted.

THE TRUNK OF THE TREE: THE ORIGINAL ETERNAL DEITY RELIGION

The deities live in a state of liberation-in-life, that is, they enjoy all attainments in a state of freedom. The deity souls have natural purity. The practical form of their purity is divinity. Their conduct is based on their original *sanskars* of divine virtues and spiritual powers. As sovereigns, they have the art of conducting themselves with great royalty and of interacting with others with respect, love, and humility. They rule as bestowers and give the rights of attainments to their entire kingdom. Their authority is the balance of love and law. All people sing the praise of the contentment they receive from their rulers. All human beings in this world, regardless of their status, are called deities, and they experience the fruits of their actions as instant happiness and power. There are no bad actions; all actions are neutral and elevated.

The deities live in both the Golden and Silver Ages. The Golden and Silver Ages are called paradise and are the trunk of the tree. This is a time when there is only one undivided world with one earth, one sky, and one ocean.

The unified principles by which the deities live are called *dharma*, which is referred to as the Original Eternal Deity Religion. The Original Eternal Deity Religion upholds the highest code of conduct. There is no name given to *dharma* that the deities would consider themselves as belonging to such-and-such a religion. Everyone is divine and lives naturally as a deity. This is why there is no need for the deities to say that they belong to a particular religion. They are not even aware of titles because there it is a divine way of life and a self-sovereign kingdom.

The deity community only exists in the trunk of the tree. The trunk is the land of truth, and it is a completely viceless and nonviolent period of the tree. The vices do not exist there, and there is no battle between good and evil. The elements of the land are pure and the souls are pure, and so not a trace of impurity or sorrow exists. Therefore, there is no need for worshipping and temples. The deities experience the rewards of the inheritance received from the Father at the Confluence Age, and so they do not worship Him, pray to Him, or remember Him.

The deities live in natural soul consciousness. At the end of their life span of 150 years, they take rebirth, and with each birth gradually use up their inheritance. After some time, when the trunk completes its growth, the omens begin to change. The deities move from their *satopradhan* and *sato* stages of purity into a *rajopradhan* stage. In this middling stage of purity, the deities begin to change their customs and systems and enter a path of searching. From being embodiments of all attainments, they begin to look outward for their fulfillment. From being worthy of worship they become worshippers and seekers.

THE EXPANSION OF THE TREE: FROM DEITIES TO HUMAN BEINGS

The human world tree continues to grow, and new souls come from the incorporeal world to play their parts. They enter the tree in their pure and righteous stage and join those original souls who have been playing their parts since the Golden and Silver Ages. This is the age when the tree is in its middle stage of purity. It is the *rajopradhan* stage of the Copper Age.

While the new souls are enjoying their inheritance of peace and happiness, the original souls are in a very slow descent. These souls do not even know that they are falling into the vices. They are not even aware that they are being influenced by the senses.

However, the change of awareness manifests in their vision and behavior with a decline in purity, peace, and happiness. These original souls come down gradually from their position of being masters and self-sovereigns. With the forgetfulness of being a soul, the third eye becomes blurred with illusion. This is called *maya*, and this illusion opposes the original identity of souls. They can no longer be called deities. They are now called human beings.

Who invokes this state of *maya*? The souls themselves come down from their position. They let go of their seat of soul consciousness, and in that empty space illusion enters. This illusion creates a duality in their consciousness. They are aware of themselves as souls, and they are also aware of themselves as bodies, that is, they are pulled by the subtle attraction of the senses. Everything the soul does under the influence of the senses becomes a mistake. The first mistake is to see themselves as bodies and not souls. Then they become attracted to the bodies of others. They become trapped in the name and form of one another, and relationships begin to tie them in attachments.

When this happens, it means that the rewards of knowledge that the original deity souls enjoyed in the Golden and Silver Ages have come to an end. At this time they begin to lose their happiness and start calling out to God, but they do not know who I am. At first they build temples to the Father and worship Me as the Purifier, performing unadulterated devotion to only One. But as their purity declines further, the worshipping becomes adulterated, and temples are built to the deities. They become worshippers of the deities and sit and worship their own worship-worthy images from ages past.

Even though they lose the insight of their third eye of enlightenment, they are still sensible. So when they bow down in front of the deities and sing their praise, they never praise them in the same way that they praise the Father. For the deities they sing, "You are complete with all virtues." But for the Father, they say, "You are the Ocean of Knowledge, the Purifier, the Bestower of Salvation, and the Innocent Lord who fills the aprons of all."

In the Copper Age, in an attempt to reclaim purity and attainments, human beings increase their devotional acts to God. They start up a variety of ways to worship, and the path of devotion begins to widen and expand. Devotion is also at first *satopradhan* and unadulterated, and then it goes through the stages of *sato*, *rajopradhan*, and *tamopradhan*.

In worshipping One God, there are some who perform intense devotion and are only concerned about being given a vision. They have such a great desire for a vision that they remain sitting there waiting for this to happen. They become totally lost in the thought of that desire and are thereby granted a vision. That is called intense devotion. Their devotion is like the devotion between a lover and beloved who, while eating and drinking, keep each other in their thoughts and remembrance. This is called *satopradhan* devotion.

On the other hand, you must have seen devotees pouring oil in lamps and worshipping and bowing down where three roads meet. That is called adulterated or *tamopradhan* devotion. There is so much difference between worshipping only the One Father as an incorporeal being of light and worshipping a T-junction intersection! Some even worship water. They say that the River Ganges is the Purifier. Who is the Purifier? How can the Ganges of water be the Purifier? That is just water! As the different ways of worship increase, souls get caught up in human images and the elements thinking that they are all forms of God.

The Branches of the Tree:
The World's Great Religions Emerge

It is at this time, when those souls who had been the original deity souls are absorbed in adulterated devotion, that the branches of the tree emerge, bringing newness to the tree. The Father explains that there are four main religions and religious scriptures. All of them begin in the Copper Age. Just see how much expansion takes place from this time!

There is the deity era in the Golden and Silver Ages, and this is followed by the arrival of the founders of the world's religions who bring messages as supports for the world. When Abraham, Buddha, Christ, and Mohammed come, their dynasties also follow them gradually onto Earth from the incorporeal region. Then there are many other paths and sects that emerge as these branches expand and form sub-branches. There is also regard for those religious founders who come later.

A religious founder is a righteous soul, or *dharamatma*. Righteous souls have incarnated in this physical world for a special task. Each one's role is essential and totally necessary. When a religious founder comes to establish a religion, it is a new soul who comes onto the world stage.

Abraham is the first religious founder to incarnate, and he lays the foundation for Islam, Judaism, and Christianity. Following him are Buddha as the founder of Buddhism, Christ establishing the Christian Religion, and Mohammed the Muslim Religion. Shankaracharya is the founder of the Sannyas Religion, which follows the path of isolation and renunciation. The name of each religious founder corresponds with his religion. All religious founders come during the Copper and Iron Ages and establish their own religions.

So just as you understand God's praise and His task, in the same way you must understand the religious founders, the righteous souls who came and departed and whose praise is sung. The religious founders pointed to God, saying that the Father says, "Remember Me," or they pointed out the importance of good and pure actions. The Father makes all these things clear by explaining them to you now.

It is now in your intellect how the variety of religions comes into existence. There is a lot of influence of devotion. It is so beautiful. People spend so much wealth on the paraphernalia of devotion, and so many dances, shows, and devotional songs are created as part of the rituals and ceremonies. They continue performing many types of devotion for birth after birth. To hold sacrificial fires and perform intense spiritual endeavors, to give donations and perform charity, and to go on pilgrimages are all part of devotion.

As the population continues to grow, there are innumerable religions that emerge from the main religions. There are even sub-branches and twigs that emerge from the main branch of each religion. The practice of devotion spreads so much. It spreads like a tree of its own, adding so many different sub-branches and leaves. As a result, there are many, many religions, and they are recognized by the different names that are given to them and their diverse ways of devotion.

On the path of devotion, too, all religions are aware that by performing good actions they receive good fruit. This is why they perform the good actions of service, making donations, and performing charity. They also understand the Law of *Karma* – that for every good action, there is good fruit, and for every mistake, the result is accordingly.

Why did the downfall take place? Body consciousness! Once body consciousness comes, all the other vices also come, and this therefore becomes the condition of the tree. To fight, to quarrel, to be bossy, and to control are all forms of body consciousness. Body consciousness is the cause of all types of discrimination of caste, color, and creed. And discrimination increases more and more to the extent that there is even discrimination based on language! At the end of the Copper Age, the whole world is an island in the middle of the ocean, and everyone is in a cage of *ravan*, the five vices. These vices cast a shadow over the tree.

FRAGMENTATION AND CONFLICT IN THE HUMAN WORLD

Even though it is the time of dusk in the life of the tree, new souls continue to come from the home, bringing with them their unique specialties. These souls enjoy their inheritance of peace and happiness and begin their journey through the four stages of life. When souls leave the home and enter the tree, they come as complete beings and join those who are already on the field of action. No matter when they enter the tree, at first souls perform actions in their powerful form and remain free from sorrow.

The tree has now become very big. Specialties, talents, and skills create variety in the different branches and leaves of the tree. The sub-branches have also continued to increase and form twigs of their own. As soon as new branches start and there is a separation, they form themselves into a group with its own unique identity, and the group calls itself a family or community. Whereas at the beginning of the tree there is just one trunk, the family of humanity, now there are so many families of branches, sub-branches, and twigs. When there are very many families, there is definitely conflict among them.

These conflicts start off as small matters, such as fighting over land and water, and each family becomes centered on taking care of the happiness and well-being of its own particular family. Fighting continues over small matters, but ultimately leads to civil wars.

There is conflict within the countless branches as well. Each branch has conflict within itself. And no matter how learned scholars are, no one listens to them and their guidance. There are so many different opinions. No one knows the way. Some simply beat their heads and continue to stumble around holding on to the thought: "Surely, God is the One who grants liberation and salvation, and so only He knows the path." However, because of not knowing the Father, of not being connected to the Seed of the tree, they have become like orphans.

It is now the Iron Age of the tree, and the human world tree extends to all four corners of the Earth. The farther the tree extends, the more distant the human world family becomes. Distance creates separation, and the one human family now becomes a fragmented family of different groups.

THE EROSION OF AUTHORITY

In looking at the Iron-Aged state of the tree, what is seen? Although every leaf, that is, every human soul, is part of the tree that has become old, the majority of the leaves have some disease on them due to which the color or form of the leaf has changed — its beauty has been lost. The authorities holding up the tree seem hollow inside and powerless. Although externally they still have their beauty, internally they seem empty — just as when something is eaten away by termites it is rotten inside, but externally you can still see its beautiful form.

The ruling authority does not have control over a kingdom. Externally it is called a kingdom, but internally, day and night, there is a lot of pull from all sides. The fire of fear and corruption is burning away. The people seated on the "chair of position" are constantly surrounded by the evil spirits of insecurity and opposition.

The authority of religion is in its external glittering form. Instead of internally being engaged in renunciation, intense remembrance, and disinterest, people are playing with the wrong types of power. Instead of having disinterest, they are caught up in conflict. Internally they are being eaten by the termites of arrogance of the self. The termites are eating away at the authority of religion, that is, they are finishing their righteous power.

In the authority of science, misgivings are apparent. Science is showing the splendor of the final time. Seeing this splendor, people think that it is heaven now and that it was hell before. However, all the tall buildings, telephones, electricity, airplanes, etc., have been invented in recent years. The scientists are very eager to increase the speed of their inventions, but the more they intensify their speed, the more misgivings they have, and this prevents them from moving at a fast speed. They have finished their preparations, and their inventions of destruction are now in the hands of those who are waiting to put them to use. They have refined everything in the material world, but are now finalizing preparations in their internal world with their own conscience.

As for the authority of the people, everyone is sitting on the pyre of worry. They are eating, they are moving along, they are performing actions, but at the same time they are constantly afraid that at any moment there will be a spark, that is, that a fire will ignite. As though in a dream, it constantly appears in their thoughts that they might be attacked at any moment by either the authority of the government, by the authority of some natural calamity, or by illness of the body. They constantly have such nightmares in their thoughts. By sitting on the pyre of such worries, they are distressed, peaceless, and experiencing sorrow, unable to see any clear path by which they could save themselves. If they go in one direction, there would be fire; if they go in another direction, there would be water. With tension all around them, they are afraid.

And finally, the authority of the natural elements is in complete disorder. In some places there is too much rain, whereas in other places there is no rain at all. The storms cause so much damage, and they come at odd times. The waves in the ocean are rising to 100 feet. The heat of the sun is so hot, do not even ask! Daily, natural calamities are increasing in force and frequency. The Earth is old and tired.

THE HUMAN WORLD TREE AT THE END OF ITS LIFE

The tree has grown to its fullest life span. The population of human beings has grown so much, and souls continue to come from the home to take their rightful places on the world tree. As people are trying to find ways to control the population, the new leaves glitter with beauty and attraction.

The human world tree has become a family of contrasts. Just see how much pomp of *maya* there is on one side and how poverty-stricken the world is on the other side. On one side of the tree, someone is having a meal worth one dollar, and on the other side of the tree, someone is having a meal worth 100 dollars. The eye of the soul – the conscience – is completely closed to wisdom and enlightenment. The tree continues to grow but in a very weak state. When a tree is weak, it is uprooted when a storm hits it. This is the condition of the human world tree.

Civil wars and natural calamities are occurring. There are torrential rainfalls, earthquakes, and famine. Death does not take time. People are developing bombs that will kill instantly. However, there cannot be complete annihilation. That is not destined to happen.

The human world tree has become a tree of thorns. It is now a world of thorns. Human beings are calling out to the Father to come and change the forest of thorns into a garden of flowers. This is why I am called the Lord of Thorns. I come and change the thorns into flowers. The thorns have become very large, and they prick with great force. People continue to hurt each other. They cause a lot of sorrow to one another. The more they desire happiness, the more their sorrow increases. The vices completely destroy the truth. Illusion and ignorance are so powerful.

There is the example of the banyan tree in which the whole tree is standing, but the foundation no longer exists. The banyan tree is absolutely accurate to describe the human world tree in its present state. At the moment, there is not the foundation of the original deity religion. The unifying spiritual principles are forgotten, and actions have become corrupt. Its whole foundation has now decayed, and yet the tree is still standing. It has no trunk, but the rest of the tree is still standing.

THE SEARCH FOR COOL SHADE

The fire of the vices is becoming even more intense in the world, and just as people cry out when there is a fire and they search for the support of coolness, in the same way human souls are crying out in desperation for a few drops of coolness. The fires surrounding them are the fire of vices; the fire of war and destruction; the fire of attachment to their own body, bodily relations, and material possessions; and the fire of repentance.

Let the fire be stilled with the power of coolness, and then on the basis of coolness they will be able to recognize the truth. The power of coolness means the power of love for the soul. The coolness of love from the mother can transform the child no matter how fiery the child may be. Love in the form of the power of coolness will transform souls burning in the various types of fires and make them cool so that they become willing and able to inculcate the truth. Before truth can be understood, there has to be coolness.

Coolness is like the shade of the tree which gives rest and comfort to the tired travelers and is cooperative at the time of need. A soul with the power of coolness is always able to give the cooperation of rest and comfort to other souls. Each one will be attracted to go to this soul and experience for even two moments the happiness and bliss that come from the shade of coolness.

The Revelation of the Father, the Seed of the Human World Tree

The wonder is to reveal the Seed in the midst of expansion. In the expansion, the Seed has become incognito. Now, it is the final stage of the tree, and the Seed cannot remain incognito any longer. I have to be revealed. It is the nature of human souls to be very much attracted to variety. However, now is the time to draw the attention of souls away from the variety and expansion and let them be attracted to the Seed.

When I come, I do not look at your caste, your creed, your country, your color, your beauty. I only see the spiritual being – the point of light – on the forehead of each of you. I only see that you belong to Me. God has to meet His devotees in order to give them the fruit of their devotion. God comes and makes those who are worshippers into those who are worthy of worship. I make those who are beggars into princes. I make those who are orphans into My children.

The Master of the World is carrying out the task of establishing peace in the world. The desire that all of you have is for there to be one world where there is love, where there is no fighting. Some of you have been working very hard for this. The time has now come for that desire of all souls to be fulfilled. Now you need to understand in what way that will happen. When the method is accurate, there will also be success.

If the essence of fighting and battling were to finish, then although weapons, etc., are available, they would never have to use them, because it is not weapons that cause damage, it is anger that causes damage. The cause of fighting and battling is anger. If anger is finished, then success is accomplished. The time for the pure desire of souls to be fulfilled has now come. Time is invoking everyone's intellect to cooperate in the incognito task of establishing peace in the world.

Planting the New Sapling

Everyone is looking for something new in the world. The Father is now planting the sapling once again. The Father comes here and starts the tree anew. The Seed has the knowledge of how the tree grows and how it is then destroyed. Those who will be the first souls in the new world are now sitting here under the old tree in order to plant the sapling of the new tree, that is, to plant the sapling of the Original Eternal Deity Religion.

These souls are sitting down below at the roots of the tree studying *Raja Yoga* and beginning the practice of intense remembrance of the Father, the Seed. They are filling the apron of their intellect with the imperishable jewels of knowledge, which they will store within themselves as *sanskars*. Everything is in their intellect exactly as it is in the Father's intellect. This is why I am called the Seed of the human world tree, and this is why they are called "master seeds." Master seeds means they are helpers of the Seed. These matters have to be understood. The Seed of the tree gives a very good explanation.

My children have to become the highest-on-high, and this is why the five vices have to be burned. If you are going to help the Seed establish the new human world tree, remove the darkness of the vices from the intellect with the fire of remembrance of the Father.

RETURNING TO THE TREE OF SOULS

All souls have to return home to their own section in the incorporeal tree of souls. Those who belong to the Original Eternal Deity Religion will return to their section. The souls who belong to the Christian Religion will return to the Christian section. Whichever religion souls belong to, they will return to that particular religion. All of those who have been converted into other religions will return to their original religion. Every soul plays its own individual role, and then, when they all return home, each soul goes to its own particular section.

The Father does not send anyone into a religion. The soul's role is played automatically according to the part latent within the soul.

In the home, the eternal religion of all souls is peace. The eternal relationship is of brotherhood, and the eternal connection is a spiritual family.

. . . You look thoughtfully at the banyan tree above you, and thank your Father, your Teacher, for this amazing story. You had never before considered the mystery of the unfolding story of the human world, and you find it more wondrous than you had thought possible. It also explains the uneasiness and sadness you were experiencing when you began this journey. What isn't clear, though, is how the souls who had known such happiness came to be enmeshed in such deep sorrow. That explanation, it seems, will have to wait for another day.

IMPLICATIONS FOR LIFE

The Father is looking at the sapling of the new tree. Do you consider yourself to be the sapling? When the old tree is diseased and completely decayed, the new tree-planting ceremony takes place through those who become the images of support. Do you consider that you are part of the roots, that is, one who becomes the foundation of the new tree? While seeing the bad conditions all around, the Father, the Seed, is merciful. I work with the roots through love and cooperation to create a new sapling. The new sapling brings peace, purity, and prosperity back to the human world tree.

SIX

THE LANDSCAPE OF *KARMA*

A s you are waiting for your sixth lesson to begin, you find yourself feeling that familiar double vision. You are now able to maintain your awareness of yourself as an eternal being of light for extended periods of time, yet at the same time you frequently experience yourself as the weary traveler in the physical world – pulled to the other actors and to the physical habits to which you have become accustomed. When your Teacher arrives, you are engrossed in this inner struggle.

He senses what is going on and settles in beside you. It is time, He says, for us to talk about the philosophy of karma. His voice pulls you from your inner absorption. You draw your attention away from the internal scenes and place it entirely on Him. You are relieved He has come and interrupted your disturbing thoughts.

Since your very first birth many centuries ago, He begins, you have been moving on the field of action. Karma is action, and it is a reflection in the outer world of the quality of awareness you have within.

When you first came from the soul world, you had a character of gold. Your thoughts were loving, happy, and peaceful, and your vision for others was always generous. The actions that you took were always elevated. You never spoke or acted in a way that was ordinary. You never raised your voice or your hand against another. Your fortune at that time was the fruit of your spiritual efforts made at this time, in the Confluence Age. Your continuous good actions, in turn, brought to you continuous good fortune, because that is the way karma works.

One of the most essential laws of the universe is the Law of Karma: for every action, there is a reaction that is in the same proportion and of the same character as the original action. So for a long time your charitable vision and benevolent actions brought you the blessings of good omens.

However, as the quality of the world began to weaken and your own character degraded, your innermost thoughts became less charitable. You found yourself seeing the weaknesses and faults in others. You were disappointed and offended by those around you. Your vision for them became ever more critical, and you began to act in the world from that degraded vision.

It is as if the innate goodness and purity of your original self was invaded by the outer material world, and you found yourself pulled into a battle between spirit and matter, between that which is eternal and innate to you and that which is temporary and acquired. He pauses to give you time to take in what He is saying.

It is true that it is a battle of sorts. You have felt it from the very beginning when you first wandered into this spiritual classroom. Even as your heart rose up to meet Him and to embrace what He was teaching, another part of you has been turning attention back to the seemingly irresistible world of matter, with its sounds and smells and dazzling scenes: up one moment, down the next; light one moment, heavy the next. You focus your gaze on Him again, and He continues.

In the early years of this battle, you retained your awareness of yourself as an eternal spirit, and your elevated nature won out over the invading distractions of the material world. As time progressed, however, you occasionally acted from this lower nature, and when you did, because of the Law of Karma, you experienced the return of those actions. It was as if your former radiant fortune began to dim.

As your journey continued, the invasions of the outer material world became more persistent, and your inner spiritual consciousness became less stable. Increasingly you looked through eyes that saw the limitation of the material world. You saw that there was not enough for everyone, that some had designs on those things and people who "belonged" to you, and you wondered if others might not have better fortune.

Eventually, in a moment that went by unnoticed, you were defeated by these baser forces of maya *and* ravan, *and you surrendered everything – ultimately even your own identity of who you really are. You took on the identity of the conquering force of matter. You believed you were the temporary physical form in which you were living and lost access to your spiritual treasures and spiritual powers.*

Your future script was being written by the karmic *accounts you were accumulating. For centuries you stumbled along acting out of your lower nature as if in a deep sleep, each action creating a reaction which bound you further to the material world and limited your freedom. You never lost your innate values and qualities, but you lost your belief that they belonged to you. You lost your access to them.*

In defeat, your connection to your spiritual nature was severed, and you were bound instead to your senses and to the world of matter. That, He says gently, is where you were when He found you.

Did He find you, you wonder. Or did you, in your deep discontent, find Him?

These dark forces that He describes seem to have won the day. There is so little evidence out there of anything other than ravan *and* maya *that you wonder what possible hope the world might have. How can this subtle spiritual force conquer the tangible horrors of* ravan? *The pandemics, the generational conflicts, the lust and greed that have consumed the world seem to be entrenched everywhere.*

Guessing your thoughts, He intervenes again to say that the pen for your line of fortune – and the fortune of the world – is now in your hand . . .

Teachings

this benevolent time of the Confluence Age, there is a chance for all human beings to understand action, interaction, and the consequences.

Each soul is in its own body. The soul is the charioteer who drives the chariot, the body. When the soul and body are together, there is the experience of happiness or sorrow. This experience takes place on the field of action, this physical world. Every soul has a part to play, and all souls have to receive the fruit of what they do. You cannot receive anything without doing something. You receive the good or bad fruit of whatever you do here in the body. Souls play their roles and express themselves through the physical sense organs of the body. No one can stay for even a second without performing actions. No one can become a renunciate of actions. The soul is not immune to the effect of action. The Law of *Karma* is absolute and universal.

ACTION AND DESTINY

God is the only soul who is beyond every action and its fruit because He is the Supreme. I do not enter the cycle of birth and rebirth, you do this.

When the Father comes at the Confluence Age, He sheds light on the meaning of *karmic* accounts. He explains how in this short leap age you can create a destiny of your choice. You can draw the line of your destiny with the pen of your elevated actions and take the rewards with you throughout the cycle of time.

The pen for the line of fortune is action. The Father teaches you how to perform elevated actions, and as a result of this you create an elevated destiny for yourself.

The present elevated life of the Confluence Age is called an effort-making life. The quality of the efforts made now is the basis of the future quality of actions and rewards. It is at this time that you go deep into the understanding of spiritual knowledge, and you inculcate the unifying spiritual principles of soul consciousness by following the supreme directions. Through this you are able to develop the power of discernment to know truth from falsehood and right from wrong.

The principles of *dharma* are inculcated by the soul through the practice of spiritual knowledge and truths, for example, having a benevolent attitude, pure vision, and soul-conscious love. When actions are connected to such principles, they are called elevated. When you perform actions aligned with your *dharma*, that is, the spiritual principles of life, and when your *karma* is balanced with your *dharma*, then the line of fortune you draw would be very long and clear. If you sometimes perform elevated actions but at other times you perform ordinary actions, then your line would be broken.

ACTION AND *SANSKARS*

Every action done leaves an imprint that is recorded as a *sanskar*. *Sanskars* are in the soul. It is the soul that has good or bad *sanskars*, and it is according to this that human beings receive a good or bad birth. Souls carry their *sanskars* with them into their next birth. These are referred to as *karmic* accounts accumulated from actions done.

For example, if someone built a college in her previous birth, she would receive a good education in her next birth. Or if someone's name is glorified in childhood, it is understood that he performed highly credible actions in his previous birth. If you perform good actions, you receive good fruit in the next birth. The reverse is also true. Some perform such actions that the *sanskars* they take with them affect them from birth, such as they are born with an unhealthy body.

Every soul has its own *sanskars* which are unique to that soul. The soul carries good or bad *sanskars* with it depending on the quality of the actions done. It is the soul that has to experience through its body the return of any good or bad action. The *sanskars* within the soul are influenced by the quality of the soul's actions. This is why whatever you do, you do that for yourself. Since you yourself do everything and you receive the fruit of that, then you understand that within every action is accountability.

ACTION AND REBIRTH

When a soul leaves the body, there is neither bondage of action with the body it has left nor bondage of action with the body it has to enter because the soul is separated from the body and is in transition. However, *sanskars* remain within the soul. The soul carries its *sanskars* with it, and its next birth is according to these *sanskars*. When it takes its next body, its connection with action continues.

Souls are faster than the speed of light. You leave your body in a second and enter the womb of the next mother. If a soul leaves its body in India and has *karmic* accounts in London, that soul will go to London and take birth there. All souls go through the cycle of birth and rebirth. Birth after birth your features continue to change. You now know that these present features will change in your next birth. Your relationships with souls also keep changing in every birth. The one incorporeal Father who is free from birth and rebirth is telling you this.

THE FIELD OF ACTION

The specialty of this physical world is action. The field of action exists here in the corporeal world, and it is here that good and bad actions are done. When the soul is in the body, you are playing a part through your sense organs on this field of action. All actions are seeds that are sown on the field. Actions are neutral, good, bad, and elevated. You plow the field with your thoughts, and you plant the seeds with your actions. As is the quality of the soil and seed, such will be the quality of the fruit you reap. This is why it is said, "As you sow, so shall you reap."

NEUTRAL ACTIONS

Every soul enters the world stage in its original stage of completion. The original *sanskars* of knowledge, powers, and virtues are innate in souls as their Godly inheritance, and their actions give fruits of peace and happiness. Neutral actions are the rewards of effort made at the Confluence Age. These actions, from ruling to eating, are in the Golden and Silver Ages. There, neutral actions are actions that are in perfect alignment with the unifying spiritual principles of the soul. There is no question of sinful actions; no souls repent for their actions.

GOOD AND BAD ACTIONS: THE LAW OF CAUSE AND EFFECT

From the Copper Age onwards, when there are *sanskars* of duality, actions are influenced by both good and bad intentions. When you step down from the consciousness of being a master, the battle begins between virtues and vices, good and evil. This battle slowly drains you of your spiritual power and makes you weak. In this place of uncertainty, your voice of conscience speaks: "Never perform any bad actions. Only perform good actions. There are good thoughts and bad thoughts. I should stop bad thoughts. God has given me this intellect to discern right from wrong. By making good effort, I can perform right actions."

However, because of your weakened position, you act against the voice of your conscience. Even against your own will, you act under the influence of the vices. Then you say: "This was not my intention, but it is my nature." From those actions, taken against the voice of conscience, bondage is already created!

When such actions take place, they leave an imprint within you as a *sanskar*. These are acquired *sanskars* based on body consciousness and the vices. During the Copper and Iron Ages, the Law of Cause and Effect is experienced. Also called the Law of *Karma*, this law is such that whatever right or wrong actions you do are accounted for in the form of *sanskars*, and the fruit of that is definitely received in the next birth.

When a soul is under the influence of its action, it means that the soul is under the influence of desire for an immediate outcome. The result is that action ties the soul into bondage, which causes distress to the self and to others. The bondage of action brings you under the influence of the limited fruit of action. The word *influence* means that one is trapped by the attachment to something external to the self. This is called actions done under the influence of body consciousness and the material world.

When there is a bondage of action, it pulls you and consumes you and you become subservient to the body, person, or situation, and this creates dislike within you. The seed of dislike is a royal form of a selfish motive. Subservience in relationships begins with a very subtle awareness of the mistakes of others and a very subtle absorption of that mistake within the self. People say when someone makes a mistake that it is necessary to acknowledge it as a mistake and to be knowledgeable in terms of understanding it.

However, in the process of understanding the mistake, it can happen that the mistake gets absorbed into your heart, your intellect, your attitude, or your words. If you absorb something negative or someone's bad behavior, will your intellect, your attitude, or your words remain clean? If even the slightest defect, flaw, or waste remains within you, you cannot remain uninfluenced. When anything bad about anyone is in your heart, then your heart cannot remain satisfied constantly. And that which is absorbed by the heart will definitely come out in words, whether it is spoken in front of the one who made the mistake or whether it is spoken in front of many.

In other circumstances, the physical senses can trap you in such a way that you do not even know that you are trapped. It then shows up in the habit of making mistakes and seeking forgiveness. There is no question of forgiveness in this. People in the world ask for forgiveness a lot. Someone would hit another, and then ask for forgiveness and think that everything is all right again. It does not take long to ask for forgiveness in that way. You cannot continue to perform wrong actions and then say, "I am sorry!" It cannot continue like this.

Everything is accumulated. Everything gets absorbed in the soul as *sanskars*. Whatever right or wrong actions you perform are accounted for, and the fruit of that right or wrong action will definitely be received, if not in this birth then in the next birth. Whatever one does, one receives the fruition of that accordingly.

Always remember that the Law of *Karma* is like an echo. If you speak about anyone's defects or anyone's mistakes, even if you consider yourself to be very sensible and responsible, this wasteful speaking is such that it echoes back. Your own sound comes back to you louder. The very powerful Law of *Karma* is such that if today you defame anyone, tomorrow someone else will defame you twice as much.

ELEVATED ACTIONS

I am now teaching you how to stabilize yourself in the stage of being a soul. This automatically brings out the original pure *sanskars* of self-benefit and self-respect and makes you a detached observer of the Law of Cause and Effect. Being a detached observer helps you to develop controlling power so that you do not come under the influence of any sense organs or any gross or subtle forms of the vices. When you sit on the seat of a detached observer, you can see clearly things about your own self as well as others, and your discernment can then be accurate. However, be your own judge, do not judge anyone else.

Whatever you do, do it after seeing and thinking about it as an observer. You will see it, think about it, and then do it. You will align your actions to the elevated spiritual teachings. The habit of checking the consciousness, that is, the quality of your thoughts before performing an action, becomes natural. The soul is reminded of its innate virtues, powers, and wisdom. Because these remain in your awareness, you are able to use them according to the time and according to the actions.

With this change in your awareness, you change your entire world of actions. You experience yourself to be double light – to be the form of light, the soul, and to be light of the burden of past actions. This experience is called being liberated in life while doing actions.

I explain the meaning and significance of life without fear, repentance, or punishment by explaining the philosophy of *karma*. If something happens, people say, "It is the will of God." You would not say this. You would say that it is the destiny of the drama. Although, according to the Law of Action, all have to face the consequences of their actions and be accountable for whatever wrong they do, I do not sit and punish you. I have come to show you the path of efforts and rewards. My part is to purify everyone. I tell you that whatever has happened, whether good or bad, was all in the drama.

KARMA AND *YOGA*

At the Confluence Age, the Father teaches the children how to perform elevated actions. You are now learning to perform actions that will make your actions neutral for many births. To perform elevated actions, you need to have the balance of *karma* and *yoga*.

In performing actions of charity and service, some people of the world say that action is *yoga*. They do not believe action to be separate from *yoga*. They think that to be a *karma yogi* means to have *yoga* with action. However, *karma yoga* means to come into action in one moment, and the next moment to be detached from doing actions. It means to be concentrated on yourself as a soul, the one who is doing the action.

Do you know how to do this exercise? If you are busy performing any action, would you be able to put a full stop to thinking about that action? Would you be able to do this, or would you continue to have thoughts of the action you were doing?

In one second, you should be able to merge the expansion of the action and become the embodiment of the essence of the soul.

A *karma yogi* is one who has relationship with actions. When you are in relationship with *karma*, then you are able to be detached and loving as the doer of the action. You will act from a stage of self-sovereignty — one with all rights and not under any kind of influences. To be in relationship with actions, you need the support and cooperation of the mind, intellect, and *sanskars*.

Any thought that enters the mind is the soil in which the seeds of action are planted. Words and actions are the expansion of the seed. By checking the thought with the power of the intellect, that is, to discern the quality of the thought, it becomes a powerful inner environment to sow seeds of action. As a result, there is easy success in your words and actions. If you do not check your thoughts, then that action may tie you in bondage.

To do this checking, experiment with the power of pure thought. With pure thought, you are able to see the successful form of whatever you want. Experiment with this on yourself and in your relationships with others. The double power of pure thought combined with love will enable you to be victorious over the vices and to perform actions that result in peace and happiness. Experiment with this in relation to your body, mind, and *sanskars*, and experience the meaning of relationship with *karma*.

To be in relationship with action means not to be one who is under the influence of the outcome of the action, but to be a master creator of the action. It means while using the sense organs to perform actions, to be detached at the same time from external influences and perishable desires. The soul should not be subservient to the outcome of actions, but it should be the master and continue to enable actions to take place. The true reality of success is in the quality of the creation of the action. The outcome is just an image that reflects this reality.

The sense organs have a strong power of attraction to immediate outcomes of action, and when the soul is influenced it becomes subservient — it is tied in bondage. As a result, the quality of the creation is affected. To be in relationship is to be beyond, to be detached. This means it is the function of the eyes to see, but who is it that is performing the act of seeing? The eyes perform the action, and the soul instructs the action of seeing to take place. This is to perform actions in a soul-conscious stage.

KARMA AND FORTUNE

Creating Fortune Through *Karma*

The Confluence Age has this blessing: For one action, there is multimillionfold return. With this awareness, you can create as elevated a fortune as you want at this time. Just as actions performed in the past determine the present quality of your actions now, the actions performed in the future will be connected with the actions performed now. The basis of constantly performing elevated actions and receiving elevated fruit is always to remember the significance of the present time and the effect it has on the future in relation to mind, body, wealth, and relationships.

Creating Fortune While Settling *Karmic* Accounts

Settling *karmic* accounts happens in three ways. First, you clear your accounts individually, personally. There is settling through body, mind, and wealth. For instance, there is settling through physical sickness and through mental suffering. Second, there is settling the account at an interpersonal level through relations and contacts. Third, there is the collective clearing of accounts through natural calamities and human-created disasters such as atomic and civil wars.

As you settle your *karmic* accounts of past actions, use the present auspicious time to master the art of elevated actions and create your fortune for the future. Put a full stop to the past and to thinking about mistakes of past actions. Understand that impure actions are performed because of the darkness of ignorance and the influence of the vices. Now you have knowledge. You are enlightened, and so you can change the quality of your actions.

Creating Fortune Through Individual Actions

To create fortune through individual actions, take love from the Father and burn and finish completely through remembrance the expansion of your *karmic* accounts.

From the beginning to the end of the world cycle, as a member of the human family tree you have come into so much expansion of your accounts. You do know the branches of your accounts, that is, the tree of expansion, do you not? There are the branches of the accounts of the body, of the relationships of the body, of being a soul in bondage to all the different facilities for the body, of bondage to all the different types of negative habits, of the physical suffering of illness — there is so much expansion!

You do not have to finish each branch individually. By connecting to the Father, the Seed, with love, settling will take place easily through the fire of love. Do not cut off the branches of accounts, but burn them. To cut the branches of accounts means to try and settle each account separately. When you cut them, after some time they begin to emerge again. What is the reason for this? You cut off the branch, but you did not burn it. Therefore, now finish the tree of the expansion of *karmic* accounts in the fire of love.

Creating Fortune Through the Body

To create fortune through the *karmic* accounts of the body means that the various illnesses of the body are not experienced as an obstacle on the path of spiritual progress or as an obstacle in receiving attainments in life.

All sicknesses of the body and the variety of heartaches are *karmic* accounts of the past, and these can create a great deal of suffering. At this time, you are settling the accounts of all your past *karmas* that remain and are sitting inside of you as *sanskars*. Whatever illness remains, it will erupt and have to be settled. You must not be afraid of that. Settle whatever *karmic* accounts you have left with the power of remembrance and love, and transform the negative account into a positive account.

No matter how sick or weak your body may be, use your mind to reflect on the power of peace and let spiritual joy radiate through your face and eyes. Nourish the body with the spiritual tablet of happiness. With your peaceful and benevolent mind, the body is nurtured. To do this for even a short period of time during your illness is healing.

Do not speak about the tale of your suffering because by speaking about it, time and power are used in that direction in the form of worry. This state of constant worrying gradually takes spiritual power away from the soul and makes it nervous. Give strength to the body with the power of the mind.

Look at your illness with patience, with a consciousness of tolerance, and with an introverted stage, and you will not tie yourself with the strings of, "Why did this happen to me?" or "Perhaps my fortune is like that." Instead, you will be able to see what is hidden behind the curtain of the illness. An illness that comes is a means of rest. Learn to deal with the pain and suffering that result from your past actions on the basis of spiritual understanding.

Creating Fortune Through the Mind

To create fortune through the mind, one needs the power of pure thought and the ability to remain cheerful by understanding that there is benefit in every scene in the drama of life.

One who has inner contentment is constantly cheerful in the mind. The Father is pleased with such souls because they use all the attainments I have given them, and so their mind is neither attracted by limited desires nor bows down to any individual or object. Their mind is in the state of *Manmanabhav*, that is, the mind easily remains in the world of the Father's love.

When you have such contentment in the mind, there will not be space for waste thoughts such as, "Why does this one say this or do this?" or "This should not be like that, it should be like this." One with a line of questions in the mind cannot remain content because time is spent in worrying about how to finish the never-ending line of questions. And even if you wish to leave the line of questions alone, you cannot, because you created it and your own creation begins to pull on you to be sustained. You have to give it your time and energy.

Therefore, control this creation of wasteful thoughts. Let there be birth control of wasteful and negative thoughts. Do you have this courage? You have to be very cautious. Many negative thoughts will come in your mind, but do not be afraid of them. Instead, be knowledgeable, be a master creator of thoughts.

While performing every action, while seeing or hearing, think, "Whatever is happening is good, and whatever is to happen will also be good." In silence, be introverted, and with the practice of *Manmanabhav*, transform a bad situation or the experience of a bad relationship into something good, and absorb that experience within the self as elevated thoughts, good wishes, and pure feelings.

Creating Fortune Through Relationships and Contacts

To create fortune through relationships with people is to make the effort for *sanskars* to meet in harmony. There should be a meeting of the hearts as well as of the minds.

A sign of fortune in relationships is that according to the need, you always receive love and cooperation from others. This will be from at least 95 percent of souls in your connection and relationship. The accounts of the other 5 percent will have to be settled. This is because although you receive love and cooperation from the majority, there also will be relationships that take the form of tests. However, these tests should not come from more than 5 percent. Gradually continue to settle your accounts with such souls with pure feelings and benevolent thoughts. When the accounts are finished, then the books will close and no old accounts will remain.

It is your responsibility to behave in relationships with understanding, love, and cooperation and not to wait for others to do so first. You be the chancellor. You act first. So settle all *karmic* accounts with people easily, and experience love and cooperation from the majority of those in relationship with you.

Your relationships with others depend on your bank balance of good and bad actions. In your interactions with others, your consciousness, vitality, vision, and understanding the relevance and purpose of the relationship will determine the quality of your actions with them. If your behavior and habits are motivated by anger, ego, greed, attachment, or blaming others, you will build up a debit account of bad actions that tie you in bondage.

If, however, your behavior is one of peace, humility, generosity, and trust, then you will constantly see and speak of the specialties of each one. You will always have benevolent feelings of making each one special, you will pay attention that your eyes are closed to seeing anyone's weaknesses or defects, and your vision is open to that which brings love and cooperation. As a result of this behavior, you will receive the instant fruit of happiness and power in your relationships. To be such an example is to perform good actions. The happiness that you create in everyone's heart becomes blessings which are accumulated in your credit account.

Creating Fortune Through Wealth

To create fortune through wealth is to have generosity of spirit and to recognize that you are responsible for however your wealth is used.

You have the spiritual wealth of knowledge anyway, but there is also the importance of physical wealth. Just as you become a trustee of the spiritual wealth of knowledge and through your efforts you accumulate an elevated income, in the same way you must become a trustee of physical wealth and use it for self-benefit and world benefit. The meaning of fortune in wealth at the Confluence Age is not that you will be a millionaire or multimillionaire, but that you receive as much as you need to eat and drink and to live simply and comfortably.

Wealth has become a source of corruption and a means of illusion. This is why wealth is called *maya*. However, wealth as a physical resource is not corrupt, it is the way it is used by human beings that makes it corrupt. When wealth is earned honestly and is used in service to humanity, it is an investment that brings benefit.

The benevolent Law of *Karma*, when applied at this time to wealth in relation to the task of God, means the task gets accomplished through many souls, drop by drop. This is a means for the future of many souls to be created. It is not just 10 or 20 souls who have to use everything of theirs in a worthwhile way, but it is many souls who are given the chance to use everything they have in a worthwhile way.

When wealth is used for spiritual service, you will neither experience any lack of wealth at the time of need, nor will you experience any struggle. Spiritual service is selfless service, and somehow, from somewhere, at the time of serving others, God, the Father, the Bestower, will make someone an instrument to provide what is needed.

Creating Fortune Through Service

To create fortune through spiritual service is elevated action. One who is fortunate never serves with the intention or desire for recognition. To serve with the desire for recognition is known as the desire for name and fame, and it is selfish. There is the difference of day and night between selfless and selfish service.

In any selfless service, if there is a real need, if the heart is true, not only will the task be successful, but also the treasure store of resources will be filled even more. Selfless service is not to be limited by resources, but to serve regardless of the resources. This is why it has been remembered that the treasure store of Shiva is overflowing. So the sign of those who serve with a true heart, who please the true Lord, is that their treasure store is overflowing. Their heart is so big that they serve with a generosity of spirit. This is the sign of those who use all their resources in a worthwhile way.

Creating Fortune Through Collective Actions

To create fortune through collective actions means that all human beings need to give their finger of cooperation at the same time to help lift this Iron-Aged mountain of sorrow.

Only the Father explains all of these secrets – that everything has now reached a state of total disorder. Now that I have come, I am reforming everything, and for that I first of all reform souls. Then, through souls, all things are reformed. Human beings are changed through elevated thoughts, good wishes, and pure feelings; the atmosphere is changed through elevated attitude; and matter is changed through powerful vibrations.

So many of My children ask, "God, why are so many dying together at once? What is the reason?" You now understand that the time of becoming complete is approaching and that the accounts of sinful actions, which have not been settled since the Copper Age, still remain. It is now time to return home. From the Copper Age onwards, whether souls were doing good actions or bad actions, if they had not completed their *karmic* account in one birth, they would be able to clear that account in the next birth.

But now, because you have reached the last scenes in the world drama – and because there is such a large account of sinful actions remaining – souls are leaving the body quickly. It becomes just a short-lived birth and death. Births to deaths are in short intervals, and through this souls are experiencing punishment. Their old accounts are being cleared in this way. At the present time, both birth and death are dreadful, and the majority of souls are suffering through this. Neither is birth easy nor is death easy. Birth is painful, and death is dreadful! This is a method for clearing *karmic* accounts quickly. Human beings are dying untimely deaths because they have to clear all their *karmic* accounts together in a very short time. This is why the cyclone of untimely death is coming from time to time.

Every elevated thought and every benevolent action is laying down the method for a new system for a better world. Create thoughts and perform actions with this elevated awareness: "Whatever I do now will become the system for the new world and will become a living memorial." Each soul can take the responsibility of becoming an instrument for world renewal. But as great as this responsibility is, so too, it is light, because I, the Almighty Authority, am with you.

EFFECT OF AWARENESS ON ACTIONS

How does the Father transform you? Do I tell you about your weaknesses, saying that you are vicious, that you are dirty? No, I remind you that you are a soul, and this elevated awareness brings you power and transforms you.

The specialty of human life is awareness. The basis of elevated action is an elevated awareness. If your awareness is elevated, your actions automatically become elevated. You would think in an elevated way and speak elevated words. Your vision, actions, and the whole inner state of being change according to your awareness. This is why it has been remembered, "As is your awareness, so is your world." I, the Father, transform your consciousness with a small shift in awareness: You are not a body, you are a soul. As soon as this transformation in awareness takes place, the soul becomes aware of itself as a true and real being and is filled with respect for the self.

You are now receiving spiritual powers and divine virtues directly from the Father in the form of an inheritance. Donate these powers and virtues through your actions with a generous heart and dispel the pain in the hearts of others. You have to come into connection with people anyway, and you also have to overcome situations – both of these things have to be faced in life. The basis of your method of dealing with such circumstances is an elevated attitude and pure feelings.

ELEVATED ATTITUDE

What is an elevated attitude? You know this very well. An elevated attitude is that of brotherhood, an attitude of soul-conscious love. It is an attitude of acceptance, cooperation, selflessness, and pure thoughts. It is an attitude of mind that does not discriminate against others. As is your attitude, such will be your vision. Your attitude will color the way you look at others. No matter what the other is like, you will see that person according to the attitude you have toward him. If someone is wearing glasses of a certain color, what will she see? She will see the world in the same color. Attitude works in the same way. Your attitude changes your vision, and your vision will change the world. So check that the foundation of your attitude is constantly elevated.

PURE FEELINGS

When you have pure feelings for a soul – or for souls of the entire world – it means you have the powerful, pure, and auspicious thoughts that there should be benefit for all. You are at the Confluence Age, and this age has the blessing that souls who make effort to have pure, loving feelings receive the instant fruit of their effort.

People desire the experience of pure feelings. However, your feelings should be powerful as well as pure. Pure feelings and pure motives are the basis of elevated action. The instant fruit of pure and powerful feelings is that any soul who comes into relationship and connection with you experiences the attainments of peace and love at that very moment. The result of your feelings of love is self-transformation and the support of transformation of souls in your relationship and connection.

If you do not have pure feelings and pure motives while doing actions, then others cannot experience the elevated meaning behind the action. Pure feelings combined with powerful thoughts travel faster than the speed of light and reach souls at far distant places, giving them the experience of love and peace. When your thoughts and feelings emerge, that soul will experience that I, the soul, am receiving peace and power.

KARMA AND TIME

Keep the importance of yourself and this time in your awareness. Every second of the Confluence Age is the time to create your reward for the whole cycle. Take every step while constantly understanding the importance of time. Time is auspicious. Time is a treasure and also a power. You have already received from Me the inheritance to become a great soul. You are great. Therefore, create every thought, speak every word, and perform every action while understanding your own greatness as well as the importance of time.

. . . Your Father pauses and looks at you. He can sense that you need time to think about today's lesson. He tells you this is enough for today, and that you will find what He has to tell you next to be very interesting. He reminds you of the magic nectar He gave you shortly after you first met: "Manmanabhav." He says that we will talk more about that when we meet again.

IMPLICATIONS FOR LIFE

Always remember that the Law of *Karma* is like
an echo. If you speak about anyone's defects or
anyone's mistakes, even if you consider yourself
to be very sensible and responsible, this wasteful
speaking is such that it echoes back.
Your own sound comes back to you louder.
The very powerful Law of *Karma* is that if today
you defame anyone, tomorrow someone else will
defame you twice as much.

SEVEN

SHRIMAT: A SPIRITUAL WAY OF LIVING

O*n the day of your next lesson, you are drawn to go for a walk beyond the parts of this vast field where you have been before. It is an exquisite morning, and you appreciate having some time to reflect on the many things you are learning in this secret school to which you have magically been admitted.*

Your thoughts go to your beloved Father and Teacher and the patience and love with which He has been teaching you. It is hard to imagine the time before you found Him, the time on the other side of the mysterious door when you stumbled in confusion along a path that seemed to lead nowhere.

Your thoughts are interrupted by finding yourself at a gateway. The beautiful gate is partway open, inviting you to enter. You step towards it, intrigued. You don't recall seeing anything quite like this before. On either side of the gate are very high hedges – beautiful, but as thick as a wall and stretching out of sight in both directions. It is impossible to see through this leafy green wall or to see over it, so you push the gate open further and walk through. You feel as if you are in a long hallway of sorts with one path going off to the left, one going off to the right, and a third continuing directly ahead before it takes a sharp turn. You decide to take the path to the right. It is so beautiful.

It is as if there is a garden within this garden running along the path. You hear a symphony of birdsongs overhead, and the air is filled with butterflies and wonderful dragonflies. The air is heavy with the fragrance of the flowers that are twining through the hedge wall. You begin to pick a few flowers to take to your Father, your Teacher. The path has taken a few turns when suddenly you seem to be at another choice point – left or right. You pause and then turn to the left. You take a few steps down the path. Perhaps if you just peer ahead you can figure out which of these offers the best way forward. Those few steps put you at another choice point: left or right again. You begin to feel nervous. You retrace your steps to the previous choice point and go to the right. There, that seems better – a straight path that goes around a bend and then, another choice point.

You are no longer thinking about how beautiful this pathway is. It must be getting close to the time for your lesson, and you are not exactly sure of which path is the way out. You haven't felt this disoriented since you were stumbling along on the other side of the door. Your heart is beginning to pound. You try to retrace your steps, but realize that you are seeing a part of this path you haven't seen before. You are sure there were not thorn bushes like these on the path you came from. You stop in your tracks and let the flowers you have been gathering drop. You can hear footsteps. Someone is here. You turn around and see your Father, your Teacher, and in this moment, your Guide, coming towards you. He is moving more quickly than you have seen him walk before, and his arms are outstretched.

You run to Him and He wraps His arms around you. You heave an immense sigh of relief. He asks you how you ended up in this maze and assures you that you are safe now. He is with you. He asks if this path feels like the confusing journey you were on in the old world you came from. How does He know your exact thoughts? And you remember the question you had then: Did you find Him or did He find you? Clearly this time, at least, He found you.

He takes you by the hand and leads you confidently forward, choosing quickly at a myriad of choice points. In a few minutes the path, which had been so daunting just moments before, opens out onto a long meadow flooded with light. In the middle of the meadow is a shimmering lake. He leads you to the edge of the lake where there are two chairs and between them a table on which is sitting a beautiful bottle filled with a golden nectar. He invites you to sit down.

Your breathing has quieted now. You are no longer anxious because He is with you. He lifts the bottle, removes the stopper, and pours you a small glass of the nectar. He sets the bottle down and tells you that you don't ever need to feel lost and confused again. This is the magic agent that can dissipate the clouds of illusion and the despair created by the forces of maya *and* ravan. *It is the life-giving nectar. It is* "Manmanabhav," *He says.*

You remember that He has told you about this magical agent before — Manmanabhav. *You lift the glass to your lips and drink some of this nectar. It tastes sweet, and as it flows down your throat, you feel it is taking all darkness and confusion away. You set the glass down and look up. He is no longer sitting but is now standing in front of you looking intently into your eyes. The life-giving nectar, He tells you, is available to you in all moments. When you remove the focus of your thoughts from everything else and place your mind on Him, He will appear in front of you. You will never have to be confused at any of the choice points along a path again. Remember Him, He tells you, and He will appear to guide you forward. And if you always remember Him, you will never be alone.*

But there are other things you can do that will help you make the right choices and create a fortunate future for yourself, He tells you. The food and atmosphere of the Iron Age have become poisoned. If you are to reclaim your sovereignty and are to dwell in the elevated Golden Age, you must begin to purify yourself. This requires great care. You must pay close attention to what you eat and drink. As you prepare your food, place your thoughts on Him so your pure, loving thoughts flow into the food. Keep your home and your physical body clean, and keep your thoughts filled with love, respect, and good wishes. Above all, He tells you, remember to use the magical agent He has given you, "Manmanabhav" *— be Mine with your mind . . .*

Teachings

directions are spiritual notes that create music in your life. Godly directions are called *"shrimat"* – elevated directions. *Shrimat* comes from the Spiritual Father for the spiritual children. To follow *shrimat* means to bring spirituality into every action. To follow *shrimat* is to see the path clearly and to show the path to others. The Father is the Bestower of Happiness and the Remover of Sorrow. He shows you the path to happiness.

As you walk this path, always have the awareness that you have the support of the Father's hand of *shrimat* and His company of cooperation. This hand and company should never be removed. This hand can only be removed when you become weak. Even one weakness can become an obstacle. Just as I have promised you, "I am with you whenever you remember Me," in the same way, *maya* in the form of obstacles is present whenever there is weakness. When you keep courage and remember God, you receive multimillionfold help in every step.

Because of love, I am now, at every moment, under every circumstance, your Guide. As your Guide, I tell you what to do, and as an Observer, I observe what you do. I give you *shrimat*, and you should therefore understand it fully. It is through *shrimat* that the whole world, including the elements, becomes elevated.

The accumulation of wrong actions in the soul results in your experiencing many difficulties. Children receive sorrow through their wrong actions and activities. It is not that sorrow is caused by the Father. I would never cause My children sorrow.

I cannot grant sorrow. I am constantly the Bestower of Happiness. I am now making you very happy. I say, "Follow *shrimat*!" On this path of knowledge, the laws – the directions – are very strict. I explain the laws, and I say, "Children, remain cautious!" However, to follow My directions is a matter of happiness, not of compulsion.

You receive *shrimat* in order to benefit the self. It is remembered that the Unlimited Father is the Benevolent One, and He comes and benefits everyone. He shows you different methods for this. Just as you are taking benefit, you have to benefit others. Every one of My children should become benevolent.

You now understand that you are becoming the most elevated of all. I am giving you such elevated directions. You are following My directions and are changing from an ordinary human being into an elevated being. Become fearless in following My directions. What is there to be afraid of? Take *shrimat* from the Father while living your life in this world. Whose *shrimat* is it? Who gives it? You now understand that I come only once in the cycle to give you *shrimat*. It is at this auspicious Confluence Age – the meeting of the path of ignorance and the path of enlightenment – that I guide you. I come and change the whole world through this guidance. I am making your intellect divine, with the power to discern truth from falsehood.

NUMBER ONE *SHRIMAT*

My Number One *shrimat* is to consider yourself to be a soul, a bodiless being, and remember Me, your Father – the Truth, Conscient Being, and Blissful One. Generally, when two things are to be joined together, they have to be of the same substance. In the same way, you can only stay in the remembrance of the Supreme Soul when you first consider yourself to be a soul. This *shrimat* is the main foundation of all the other directions. Repeatedly pay attention to this aspect, and you will find all the other directions to be easy. The Purifier Father shows all the children the same method. This method is called *Manmanabhav* – Oh soul, remember Me, your Father. The more love your intellect has, the more you are able to understand and practice this.

CODE OF CONDUCT: THE LINE OF SAFETY

The original religion of the soul is peace and nonviolence. The soul must now return to its original state of being completely nonviolent. There should be nothing violent in your thoughts, words, vision, or actions. As much as possible, do everything with love and in peace. The *sanskars* that you fill yourself with now will continue for many births. Whatever you accomplish, you must have no ego about it. Do not listen to, speak of, or look at negative things. Let your every thought, word, action, and dream be accurate and wise. Let every moment be meaningful in the daily timetable.

Shrimat is only one word, but it has very great significance. *Shrimat* tells you what thoughts to have, how to see, how to speak, with which consciousness to perform actions, and how to eat food. You even receive *shrimat* about how to sleep! *Shrimat* sets the code of conduct with which to check your daily chart. The code of conduct is the line to keep you safe on your spiritual path. So check: What is your consciousness, your attitude, your vision? Every aspect should be within the line of the code of conduct.

PRACTICAL SPIRITUAL PRINCIPLES OF LIFE

The practical principles of *shrimat* are based on the spiritual treasures you receive. These treasures are knowledge, powers, virtues, the elevated time, and elevated thoughts. These spiritual treasures are given to you in trust, to be used in a worthwhile way in order to reclaim your self-sovereignty. The more honest you are in using these treasures, the greater the protection you receive. As trustee of all My treasures, use them according to the Father's directions. The understanding that you are a trustee of these treasures connects the soul to its original value and gives it strength to practice *shrimat*.

Company

Stay in the company of the Father and be colored by truth. No one can change the color of truth. Go to sleep in the state of remembrance, that is, in remembrance of the Father. To be colored by God's company of truth is to receive will power. Do not become deceived by bad company. Keep your head clear and your heart clean, and interact with everyone with great tact. You may have to live among thorns, but you must stay as a flower. Do not become a thorn yourself. Thorns prick and cause sorrow.

Food

Whatever food is put into the body has an impact on the soul. Take precautions with your food and observe a high level of physical and mental cleanliness in the preparation and ingredients. There is benefit in eating pure food. The body is nourished, the mind is calmed, and the intellect stays pure and powerful.

Your food should be *sattvic*. A *sattvic* diet is the purest diet most suitable for a *Raja Yogi*. It is totally vegetarian, cooked with love in remembrance of God.

Be detached from the body while feeding the body, and the food will be absorbed in a peaceful way and you will enjoy the food. Eat to live, do not live to eat. By eating in remembrance of God, the food becomes pure. Through the power to digest, the food becomes strength in the form of blood for the body. The food does not remain separate from the body. Prepare food and eat it in silent remembrance. However, sometimes you are in situations where you yourself cannot prepare food. No matter who has prepared that food, you can purify it with the power of remembrance.

Senses

Hear no evil! Listen only to pearls of wisdom. This brings benefit. Let the rest enter one ear and leave through the other.

Speak no evil! Be introverted. Speak softly, speak sweetly, and speak less. Do not allow unkind words to emerge from your lips. Stones should never emerge from your lips. Do not hurt anyone's feelings.

See no evil! The eyes are windows of the soul. Make your eyes civil. Look with civil eyes, not with criminal eyes. This means look at others as souls and respect the souls for their unique specialties.

Thoughts

Thoughts created in the incorporeal, soul-conscious stage are full of purity and wisdom. By paying attention to thoughts, your words and actions will automatically be checked. Keep the slate of your mind completely clean and clear of anything wasteful and disturbing. No matter if storms do enter your mind, do not let them influence your actions. Storms come to test you, not to defeat you. If you do not battle with the storms of *maya*, how could you become powerful and victorious?

I consider the treasure of thoughts to be the most precious treasure. Therefore, become the incarnation of economy with your treasure of thoughts. When you are economical in your thoughts, that is, when you save your thoughts from being wasteful, you will automatically be economical with all your other treasures. Let there be quality, not quantity, in your thoughts.

Words

When you first consider yourself to be a soul and then speak to others, your words are egoless and are filled with power. Words are like sharp arrows and carry great impact. When used in the right way, they can hit the target with precision, as words of wisdom that give a meaningful experience. However, if the arrow of words is used in the wrong way, it can pierce the heart and hurt the feelings. Never cause trouble for anyone with your words. Value your words like precious pearls.

When one person says something in anger and the other person responds likewise, that is like a clapping with the mouth – a war of words. If one person says something but the other one remains quiet, then everything becomes quiet. This is what I teach.

Make effort to maintain a stage of equanimity in happiness and sorrow, in praise and defamation, in respect and disrespect. If anyone says wrong things or becomes angry, just remain quiet. Do not take the law into your own hands. Do not waste your energy.

Let there be great royalty in your way of speaking and in your exchange of words. Words should give the donation of life to others. They should show the path to peace and happiness.

Actions

Before performing any action, have the awareness of *shrimat*. When actions are performed on the basis of *shrimat*, they are viceless and they make your life elevated. To understand yourself to be an imperishable soul is the right understanding for doing actions. To consider yourself to be a perishable body is the wrong understanding for doing actions. Make the practice firm that you are a soul. "I, the soul, am acting through the body." Offer every action to the Father for guidance before doing it. Perform good, right actions and be fearless. Through your every action, give the donation of virtues.

The Father is merciful. I give you *shrimat* for what you have to do: If you do not follow My directions, you are being merciless to yourself. Have feelings of mercy for the self. Accurate mercy is based on knowledge and does not allow feelings of fear to emerge. You may be afraid of performing sinful actions, but there should never be fear of the Father.

Relationships

You have to live in relationship with others, yet remain beyond your body and bodily relations. To remain beyond means to remain detached from attitudes of your past experiences. While looking at another, remain aware of the soul. Connect to the person at the soul-conscious level. While interacting with your physical relations, you can then maintain a spiritual relationship. Cleanliness in attitude means contentment in relationships. A clean attitude nurtures honesty and trust.

When you look at one another with a soul-conscious vision of brotherhood, there will be respect and understanding. You will have the consciousness, "All of us are souls playing our parts through the bodies." The main teaching you are given is to have a great deal of spiritual love for each other as souls. All of this is understood with your intellect, but because you become body conscious you no longer have that love for each other, and you continually find fault with one another. When you are soul conscious, you never find fault with anyone – you have a great deal of love and tolerance for each other. Then the saying, "We are all brothers," will become practical. As souls, you are now true brothers because you know your Father.

Time

Do not waste your time! Your pure, elevated thoughts transform time. Always keep in your consciousness that the present time is a spiritual treasure. Use the treasure of time to make not only every day but also every moment the greatest. When time is used in a worthwhile way, it cooperates with you.

You are an instrument for bringing into being the time of the golden dawn. You are victorious because you are the embodiment of the blessing of being immortal. You now know that the form of the soul is not influenced by either time or death. This is why you should not act under the compulsion of time, but follow My directions and be prepared before the end of the cycle of time.

Powers

Spiritual powers are your weapons on the field of action. They are also your cooperative arms. In order to benefit the world, become completely full of the treasure of all spiritual powers [see Pages 15, 115]. Check whether you have internalized all the powers or whether a particular power is missing. If you have any weakness, find the cause and use the spiritual powers to remove it. *Maya* in the form of illusion will use your weakness in order to deceive you. If not removed, that particular weakness will defeat you. Therefore, do not allow any weakness to stay within you. A great and brave spiritual warrior is always victorious because that one has the authority of all spiritual powers and is skilled in using these powers as a force to remove the darkness of ignorance.

Virtues

In your original form, you are described as perfect and complete with all virtues. Through the process of birth and rebirth, you forgot that virtues are your original state of being. When you are able to remember this, you can emerge the virtues that you used to have naturally. You know what these virtues are. The more soul conscious you are, the more these virtues will emerge. Many speak of virtues, but very few realize these virtues are original to you. If you do not know about them, how can you use them? Virtues are the most elevated gifts that you can offer to others.

When you meet others, offer them the gifts of love, peace, and happiness. Share the gifts of all virtues through your actions. At the present time, there is the need to become the embodiment of virtues, such as patience, kindness, and compassion. Have the thought constantly of becoming the embodiment of virtues by sharing virtues with others and making them into the embodiment of virtues as well.

Two Paths on the Soul's Journey: Descending, Ascending

The Father explains to you the meaning of the stage of descending and the stage of ascending. There is the path of ignorance, which is called the descending path, and there is the path of knowledge, which is the ascending path. I have come to make you ascend. I am giving you directions for what to do so that your intellect can become wise.

It is not that another person can help you in this. You have to help yourself. Certainly, some people's intellects are weak and other people's intellects are sharp. However, if you do not have *yoga* with the One who is ever-pure, then your intellect will not receive strength, that is, the battery cannot become charged. The intellect will not have the power to make accurate decisions. Then neither would you accept My directions nor would you be able to imbibe My teachings.

Descending

There are many types of directions. As many mouths as there are, there are that many dictates! You receive dictates of so many – mother, father, brother, sister, teacher, *guru*, etc. The soul is influenced by the opinions of others. On the path of ignorance, it is common for people to become angry and to give sorrow, to have arrogance of their achievements, and to make others feel subservient. To be influenced by any vice means the soul comes under an external influence.

This influence draws the soul into the shadow of another, and you begin to follow the dictates of that person. You should not blindly follow the dictates of others whether negative or positive.

For example, a negative influence happens when there is interest in listening to gossip about others. This interest makes you into a dustbin for other people's garbage. Whatever gossip they have, they will come to you because they know that you are available to listen. You collect little by little within yourself the rubbish of gossip, and this creates a difference in your behavior and activity. Whenever you are with the person who was gossiped about, there will be a feeling of heaviness, and this will affect your way of thinking about that person. You begin to think of what you heard about that person, and your intentions toward that person change. The opinions of others cause you to descend from your seat of self-respect.

To see, hear, and think about things that create an upheaval inside of you is wrong, for it interferes with your intentions and it wastes your time and energy. To look and listen with feelings of benevolence is your responsibility. When you see and hear, do so with the intention of bringing benefit.

There is also the influence of following the dictates of your own selfish desires. These dictates come in the form of "I" and "mine" and body consciousness. To do something with a selfish motive is to follow the dictates of your own mind. One is to do something with selfish motives, and the other is to do something with benevolent feelings. Such benevolent feelings come from having thoughts of your original and eternal self.

This Iron-Aged community is unhappy because it is trapped by the chains of the five vices, *ravan*. My directions are breaking those chains. You may carry on with your life – your business, work, travels – you can do anything you want. However, simply follow My directions. Otherwise, the influence of the opinions of others or the dictates based on your own selfish desires will repeatedly make you fall.

Ascending

On the ascending path, I, as your Teacher, give you knowledge. As the Guide, I explain how to imbibe the knowledge, and I emphasize the importance of following directions. To the extent that you follow *shrimat*, you constantly experience being uplifted in a natural and easy way.

The first sign of ascending is a feeling of contentment in the heart and mind. This would not be superficial but a deep feeling of inner contentment. You would experience yourself to be light. Following *shrimat* gives the power to find solutions and removes the habit of creating reasons and excuses.

The second sign of ascending is faith in the intellect. Only when you have faith are you able to follow *shrimat*. The sign of faith is victory. Victory comes from having four types of faith: 1) To have faith in the Father and to understand *shrimat* accurately, to accept it, and to follow it; 2) To know and accept your elevated fortune with complete self-respect; 3) To know the family of humanity accurately and to accept that you are part of the family; 4) To recognize the Confluence Age as the most auspicious time in the entire cycle – and to move with it.

The third sign of ascending is the recognition of your elevated self and the awareness of the highest state of each one. This is your original nature. The original *sanskars* are of being a donor, a benefactor, and of being merciful. This will free you from the influence of your old, impure nature and *sanskars*.

The destination is very high. You have now received a loving intellect to discern between what is right and wrong. You should not mix anything into *shrimat*. If there is any disturbance in your intellect or mind and if there is not clarity, then understand that there is a mixture of some kind within your own thoughts. Remove the cloud of the mixture and see the clear path of ascent.

THE FOUNDATION OF *SHRIMAT*

The foundation of *shrimat* is purity and truth. How accurately you follow *shrimat* is based on your own realization of these two pillars of life.

Purity

When I come, I see that you have completely lost your way. You have become very confused. It is as though you have been lost in a fog. You are trapped in a huge forest of forgetfulness. I have come to remove your confusion. Whether or not you yourself realize your own value, I see your worthiness and specialty and have made you belong to Me. You receive this vision of love from Me, the eternal Ocean of Love, and you claim the right to be loved eternally. With this love, you recognize purity, that is, you recognize innocence to be your original state of being. You forgot this. Now, once again, I come to remove the curtain of extreme darkness and to reveal to you the light of your original pure self.

In your heart there is the subtle remembrance that purity is the very first basis of your spiritual life. Purity is the method to be able to experience true love. The more you adopt purity in every way, the more you will become worthy. Those who adopt the special virtue of purity as their eternal virtue will be able to recognize their own goodness and value.

I give you this direction. If you want to become worthy of being a charitable soul, the first thing is to remain pure. You first came to this world pure, and you have to return home pure. There is now a need for purity in the world. The more spiritual progress you make, to that same extent, purity would be seen in your attitude, vision, words, and behavior.

Adopt manners of purity and be attentive at every step. To be in the awareness of your original state of purity and to reform your character, examine yourself and ask, "Does my character make anyone sad or unhappy? Do I become body conscious in my interactions with others?" Check yourself properly. A *yogi* is one who takes the vow of celibacy. Celibacy is not just physical abstinence. It is a commitment to purity at all levels of life. Purity frees the soul from all its gross and subtle burdens.

The true joy of a *yogi's* life flows from the nectar of divine knowledge and from the bliss that comes from the purity that lies in the closeness between the soul and the Supreme Soul.

The complete form of purity means to become equal to the Father in your stage. This stage is to be incorporeal in your form, egoless in your nature, and viceless in your *sanskars*. Purity is to constantly have Me as your Companion and to stay always in the company of spiritual truths.

Truth

It is said that good company takes your boat across and bad company sinks it. It is also said that the boat of truth may rock, but it will never sink. Truth never fluctuates; it is always stable. It is the power of truth that is called *reality*. There is greatness in the power of truth. Importance is given to the truth. Do you very clearly understand that truth, that greatness?

The special method in following *shrimat* is based on the realization of truth. The first realization is to check the truth in the knowledge of the self, which is the form of the self. What is your true form, and what did you used to believe it to be? Therefore, the first truth is the form of the soul. You have been given by your true Father the true knowledge, true attainments, true remembrance, true virtues, and true powers. By having the truth, you attain fearlessness. Those who speak the truth would be fearless. They would never be afraid of anything.

Company colors the soul. Remembrance is called company. God's love is the special basis for remembrance. If the experience of God's love is lacking in your life, then life without love is no longer enjoyable; it becomes a dry life. It is God's love that is constantly with you in life and remains cooperative with you as your companion at all times. I cooperate with every soul in giving them love and regard. Where there is love and the company of the truth, everything becomes very easy and simple and you are able to follow *shrimat* easily.

It is only by staying in the company of the true Father, the true Teacher, and the true Guide that you receive the power to transform. Without the company of the truth, weak souls cannot become strong. I am your Eternal Companion. I am the Companion who will never deceive you. I will always be with you. The more you remain in the company of the truth, the more you benefit, the more powerful you become, and the more happiness there is. It is in the company of the truth that you find once again the true worth of your self-respect.

All souls create their fortune of liberation and liberation-in-life with the power of truth. Nature – the natural world – returns to its highest state of truth, the *satopradhan* state, and this world becomes the Golden Age. Truth is like a philosopher's stone. Just as a philosopher's stone changes iron into gold, the power of truth makes souls, nature, time, and everything else – all relations, *sanskars*, food, and interactions with others – *satopradhan*. That is, everything moves back to its highest state of truth.

. . . While you have been sitting and listening to your Father, the sun has traveled across the sky and is now moving toward the horizon. Your memory of being lost in the maze has faded, and you are filled with a feeling of safety and quiet hopefulness.

You realize what a rare gift these elevated directions are. His loving vision of you and His promise to guide you whenever you think of Him are precious beyond words. Manmanabhav, the magical agent He has brought for you, is an assurance of His elevated guidance and companionship at every moment. He may have found you, but your heart swells with happiness as you take in the awareness that now you never need to be lost – or found – again.

IMPLICATIONS for LIFE

One who takes every step following
elevated directions easily and automatically
claims the blessing of success in every action.
As are the directions you follow, so is the
destination you reach.

EIGHT

RAJA YOGA: THE STUDY AND PRACTICE OF TIMELESS TRUTHS

On the morning of your eighth lesson, you are up early and decide to go for a walk. You find you do some of your best thinking when you are walking. In the time that has passed since your experience in the maze, you have felt lighter and more contented than at any other time in memory. The inner battles with ravan and the storms of maya seem to have subsided, and you have found yourself moving easily through your days, seeing the events around you with remarkable clarity and knowing precisely what action to take in each moment.

You are sure it is the magical agent that has caused this, with its ability to take away all heaviness and confusion and to bring your Father immediately into your presence. You have drunk of this sweet nectar often since that day and have finished the nectar you received. Today you are planning to ask Him for more.

You follow a path that winds up a high hill to a part of the garden where you have found your Father before. When you arrive, you see that He is sitting cross-legged on a grassy knoll, facing away from you. He does not seem to have heard you come up, so you quietly circle around Him at a little distance. You see that His eyes are open, but He doesn't exactly seem to be looking at anything on the horizon. It is as if He is looking at some inner scene.

You sit down not too far away to wait for Him to stir. In moments He turns to you and smiles. You get up and move closer to Him. He seems present now. His attention has left where it was and is now focused on you. He knows you have been using the magical agent He gave you and asks you how it has changed you.

You are excited to talk about this, and you tell him how transformative it has been and how you are ready for more. He smiles and nods. He knew it would be valuable to you in those inner battles with ravan *and in those moments of outer confusion when you were paralyzed by* maya *and the choices in front of you.*

Setting aside the subject of the magical agent, He says that it is time for your eighth lesson. Today, He says, you will learn about Raja Yoga. *He asks if you remember when He told you about your lost kingdom and His promise to you that if you would study with Him, that He would help you to reclaim this kingdom. You nod: Yes, you of course do remember.*

Before you lost your physical kingdom, He continues, you lost your inner wealth. Your mind became enslaved to the world of matter and drew you away from your elevated seat and your sovereign throne. It was as if your mind was the steed on which you were riding and it ran away with you on its back. The magical potion gives you the power to rein in the mind and lead it to the most elevated place from where you can see clearly.

Yes, that's right, you think. It is as if the storms of emotion and confusion subside in those moments, and you regain your equilibrium and calm. It truly is magic.

He asks what you would think if He told you that you did not need the magical agent. A sense of alarm and confusion sweep through you. What does He mean? He Himself told you that this agent would protect you, and now He is suggesting that you may not need it.

He tells you that in drinking the magical potion, you have been given the experience of elevated awareness, the sensation of what it is like when you have mastery and authority over your senses. You have been able to see how naturally the world around you cooperates and supports you when you are in this state of mastery. In this state you have experienced deep contentment and the heights of happiness. This is the state of awareness of a true sovereign, He says. In this state you can see the past, the present, and the future together. You know what actions and circumstances in the past have produced this moment, what action you should take in the present, and what future that action will create. You see others, not as the physical beings standing in front of you, but as the eternal spiritual beings residing within. You have high regard for each one, knowing their innate goodness and feeling your kinship with each one.

Yes, yes, everything He is saying is exactly right. This is the experience you have been having since using the magical agent. It has been remarkable, and it is the state you want to stay in always.

This elevated state of awareness, He says, is the result of your being linked to Him. It happens naturally when you are able to shift your inner experience of who you are from the physical being of matter to that of being the eternal, conscient being of light, the living star, and link to Him.

He stops talking and looks at you deeply in silence. As you look into His eyes, you feel yourself lifted by His loving vision of you. Your awareness of the scene around you – and even of your own body – falls away, and you are suspended in space and time. Moments pass . . . or maybe ages pass . . . eventually He releases you with His eyes. The world comes back into focus . . .

107

Teachings

108

 *is a study and*

practice that takes place on the field of action. Through this study and practice, human beings return to their eternal and original state of being.

When you were masters of the world, you had the highest and purest form of spiritual power. Now, after going around the entire cycle, you, the soul, have no power left. In order for you to regain your spiritual power, you are once again studying *Raja Yoga*. Power does not mean that you conquer your enemy through a physical battle or other forms of violence. No, you are nonviolent, and the spiritual strength that you receive is from the spiritual Father. You win the battle over the vices of *ravan* and the illusions of *maya* with this spiritual power.

THE TEACHER OF *RAJA YOGA*

I look at you, My child, and see the soul, and you, the soul, also understand that the Supreme Soul, who is your Father, is seeing you. The Father looks at the bodiless form, the form of the soul. I see My long-lost, now-found-again child. I look at the eternal and original stage of the soul. I look at the soul with a spiritual vision. This is called spiritual consciousness.

Your Father becomes your Teacher, and I am now personally in front of you and am teaching you. You know that I do not take any fees. I neither read from a book, nor do I study from any scriptures before speaking. It is I, the Teacher, the Supreme Soul, who teaches you *Raja Yoga*. Who is listening? It is you, the soul.

The Teacher speaks to the soul, and the soul listens to the Supreme Soul. This is soul consciousness.

I teach you with so much love. I am the Ocean of Love and the Bestower of Happiness. You receive so much happiness from Me. I understand how much knowledge you have and how much intoxication of *yoga* you have. I also know how virtuous each child is. The Teacher must know this to keep a record of every student.

I am the Ocean of Knowledge, I am giving knowledge to you, and your memory is awakening. I am teaching you knowledge and *yoga*, and it is through these teachings that you remember who you are, who I am, and your role in the world drama. Unless you have the faith that you are a soul, you are unable to remember this.

A Student of *Raja Yoga*

You are a student, and you are called a *Raja Yogi*. A *Raja Yogi* is one who is an embodiment of three types of awareness: awareness of the self, awareness of the Father, and awareness of the knowledge of the world drama.

A School for Souls

This is a spiritual university. It is a university for the world. This is God's University. It is only at this time that God opens a spiritual university where everyone can study to become elevated human beings. At no other time is there such a university. This is also called a school for the souls who come to study to become self-sovereigns.

The character of a person can be seen from what that person studies. This study makes your character divine. When you study this knowledge, your character is molded accordingly.

Everyone — including the elderly, youth, and children — has a right to study this knowledge. You only receive this spiritual knowledge once; you cannot receive it at any other time. It can only be received at the Confluence Age. I, the Ocean of Knowledge, am having a heart-to-heart conversation with you. This study is unlimited, so pay a lot of attention to what you are studying. You should study regularly. I give you new and deep points every day.

You have to study this knowledge accurately and with discipline. The more effort you make to imbibe the knowledge, the more benefit you experience. Those who have faith in their intellect and study well race ahead. The practical proof of this knowledge is your life. Continue to study for as long as you live and do not get tired.

Understand very clearly the difference between knowledge and *yoga*. To study, understand, and speak is to be knowledgeable. To practice *yoga* on the basis of experimenting with knowledge is to be powerful. Being powerful is to imbibe the knowledge and to be the embodiment of what you know. The contrast between knowledge and *yoga* should be clear in your intellect. When I say, "Remember Me," that is not knowledge, it is practice. It is My direction to be in union with Me and to be in relationship with Me. *Yoga* means remembrance of the Seed. Knowledge means to know the method of *yoga* and the details of the world genealogical tree.

THE FOUR SUBJECTS OF *RAJA YOGA*

Raja Yoga is a study of four subjects: knowledge, *yoga*, inculcation into daily life, and service. Those who have the practice of studying every day are the ones who are able to pass with honors. To pass with honors means you claim three certificates: a certificate from the self, one from the world, and one from God.

Knowledge

This knowledge of *Raja Yoga* is for the whole world. Knowledge is received to be able to practice the pilgrimage of *yoga*. This is a subtle and main aspect. This knowledge is not about any physical drill, chanting, or breathing. I am explaining to you the secrets of the Creator and the creation, which is the introduction to Myself and the history and geography of the world. I am reminding you of what you are eternally, what you were originally, and what you are now. I also explain the deep significance of the philosophy of elevated action, neutral action, and sinful action.

I am explaining to you that you now have to return home. This world is physical, and that world is spiritual. This world is a huge stage on which you act out your part as a human being. That world is the silent home where you reside as a soul and I reside as the Supreme Soul. It is only when the play is over that all souls can return home. However, you have forgotten your way back. I have come to hold your hand. I am holding your hand of the intellect and taking you home. You understand that you are impure and that you have to become pure.

Yoga: Remembrance/Meditation

Life is a game of forgetting and remembering. Now is the time to remember the Father, the One to whom you have been calling out for so long. The main thing that the Father teaches you is the pilgrimage of remembrance. Be in My remembrance and return with Me. This is the pilgrimage you are on.

The more you stay in remembrance, the more love you receive, the more you are able to imbibe the nectar of knowledge and follow My directions, and the more your sins are absolved. The more you remember the Father, the higher your mercury of happiness rises.

For remembrance, consider yourself to be a soul and be in soul consciousness. Do not remember bodily beings, objects, or possessions. Remember: "My Father is the Benefactor, and I am His child." Once you have imbibed this habit, then even when you are sitting in a plane or a train, you would have the internal attention to stay in remembrance.

The early morning hours are very good for remembrance. You can enjoy yourself a lot at that time because everything is peaceful and quiet, and the atmosphere is very good. Between 3 a.m. and 5 a.m. is a first-class time. Throughout the rest of the day, you should not make it a habit of only sitting down for remembrance because you can have remembrance while walking and moving around, too. If you are unable to have remembrance while walking and moving around during the day, then sit for special remembrance in the evening so that you can at least accumulate some strength.

Moving Inward

Be introverted, be silent, and consider yourself to be a soul. There is no need for you to say anything. Think of yourself as a tiny point of light seated on the throne in the center of your forehead. This is called being soul conscious. The way to strengthen and sustain the stage of soul consciousness is to have pure thoughts and good wishes and to use the power of the eye of the intellect, the third eye.

Moving Upward

Because you are now in your body, you have to become a spiritual traveler. It is you, the soul, that travels. Where do you go? While you are still sitting here on the throne of your body in the center of your forehead, your intellect remembers your Father and your home.

When I say "Remember Me," you can understand for yourself that your Father is the Supreme Soul. I am the same One to whom you have been calling out. I now say that you are My child and I am your Father. Have *yoga* with Me alone. Souls are eternally My children, but they have forgotten Me.

The first thing that souls call out for is peace. You ask how you can have peace of mind. Peace is the original religion of the soul. The soul experiences peace in the land of peace, the sweet home. That is also called the land of silence, where there is no noise or sorrow. You must now consider yourself to be a soul and remember Me in the home.

The home is also called the land of liberation. You now have to go back to your abode of liberation. You do have to go there anyway, even if you do not remember Me. However, you remember Me in order to destroy the burden of sins on your head. It is by staying on this pilgrimage of remembrance of the Father in the home that your sins will be cut away and the soul will be cleansed. All souls return home as pure souls.

You have been seeking attainments through many relationships with physical beings. Now, through having *yoga* with One alone, you can experience all attainments through all relationships with Me, such as Mother, Father, Teacher, Friend, Companion, Beloved, etc. Each relationship fulfills a specific need in the soul and brings a feeling of contentment.

For example, remembrance of Me as the Comforter of Hearts opens the soul to the power of love. Love is a very great power. When you open your heart to the Beloved, you receive the power to heal. The one who has all relationships with

Me tastes the sweetness of all attainments. Then there is no need to go from soul to soul seeking attainments. When the Father is with you and is combined with you in your thoughts and feelings, you experience power in your every relationship with Him. This is what is meant as experiencing all relationships in the Father's company and remembrance.

With the attainments you would get from all the relationships with the Father, you would give generously to others, and others would also experience these attainments in their relationship with you.

Moving Forward

I have brought heaven for you on the palm of My hand. Remember the new world, which is your kingdom. The eye of the intellect should see it. This is called divine vision. I am making your intellect clean. You now have a divine intellect. No one except God can change you from one with a stone intellect into one with a divine intellect.

You claim the sovereignty of the world with the power of *yoga*. No one can claim the sovereignty of the world with physical power. The whole kingdom is being created here through your becoming a self-sovereign. The inheritance you receive is of peace, purity, and happiness. The spiritual treasures you receive are knowledge, powers, virtues, and blessings. I give you knowledge as well as the most elevated directions on how to create the most elevated heaven again. You should keep it in your intellect that you have created heaven many times before. You claimed your kingdom many times, and then you lost it many times. Continue to turn this around in your intellect in silence, and it will be as clear as if it were just yesterday.

Sweetest child, I am establishing heaven for you. You are the one who will go and live there. You are now facing that direction. Keep your eyes on your destination.

Inculcation Into Daily Life

You study and inculcate the teachings. Just as the sun is very bright and thereby dispels darkness and gives light to others, in the same way, you should pay attention to remaining stable as the embodiment of all spiritual powers and virtues. But not just for yourself. By being an embodiment of the light of knowledge, you also are able to dispel the darkness of others.

Put a full stop to everything that has happened up to now. Do not think about what happened in the past. When you worry about the past, you waste your time, energy, and thoughts. A great soul is innocent of anything wasteful and of vices. Let those *sanskars* of greatness emerge now. Become an embodiment of innocence of anything wasteful, such as wasting your time, breath, words, and actions. This force of waste finishes the consciousness of truth. When you become innocent of any waste, you will automatically experience divinity and give others that experience, too.

Become introverted and examine yourself. See what your character was like throughout the day. By keeping a chart, you can reform your character. Check everything: "Do I become body conscious? Is my vision spiritual? Is the look on my face constantly cheerful, or does it fluctuate? Are my awareness and attitude spiritual only when I am sitting in remembrance and when I am doing special service? Or do my face, awareness, attitude, and behavior stay special even while I am carrying on with my regular work? Is my way of speaking and acting spiritual?"

Check yourself, but do not engage yourself in checking others. It is very easy to check others, but it is very difficult to check yourself. By keeping a chart, you will remain cautious and you will not make mistakes. If you repeatedly make mistakes, you should understand that you yourself are going to incur a great loss. To check, change, and inculcate is to become the embodiment of success.

Service

The service that world benefactor children do is spiritual. They study the knowledge and teach others. They give to others the introduction of the Father and show others the path to peace and happiness. The great thirst of souls is to experience peace and spiritual love. Children create a variety of new plans, new projects, and new methods to bring spirituality into practical life. Through this they sow the seeds of self-transformation by using all their assets – mind, body, wealth, time, and energy. They also establish close contact with souls of different varieties of professions and backgrounds, and together they work in cooperation towards world benefit.

You can be a world server. The crown of responsibility of world service is being offered to you. Give the message that the Father has come to everyone in all four corners of the world. On the one hand, be a very humble world server, and on the other hand, be the embodiment of spiritual truths. When you serve in a state of soul consciousness, you are called a spiritual server.

You also must pay attention to the balance of self-progress and expansion in service. Spread into the atmosphere the spiritual vibrations of the stage of the self – of being bodiless, detached and loving, and of having a generous heart. This is the method for a fast speed in service. Before serving others, if you are accurate in this method yourself, you will be enriched by the service you do. This natural practice will change nature, whether it is the nature of human souls or the nature of matter.

The Father keeps an account of three types of service for all His children: service through the mind, through words, and through actions.

Service Through the Mind

Through your mind, give whichever power a soul needs, that is, with a pure attitude and through vibrations, donate the powers to that soul – give cooperation. Your pure attitude of mind is of kindness, help, and encouragement, and this ignites the light of enthusiasm and courage in others. You can spread vibrations all around and create a powerful atmosphere while sitting in one place. It is the finger of your elevated determined thought – "I must make the world elevated, happy, and peaceful" – that helps lift the unhappy world of the Iron Age and transform it into the happy world of the Golden Age.

Just as you share knowledge with the language of words, in the same way, use your power of silence and language of your eyes to give others an experience. The power of silence is a much more elevated power than any physical way of serving. The power of silence is your special spiritual weapon. With this power you can make the peaceless world peaceful.

Now, according to the changing times, become a soul who experiments with the power of silence. Just as you create feelings of love and cooperation in souls with your words, in the same way, stabilize in the stage of benevolent wishes and pure feelings and make the feelings in others elevated. Just as a flame can be ignited with another flame, your powerful good wishes can ignite elevated feelings in others.

Service Through Words

Your service is that of giving spiritual knowledge through words. Your words should be such that they would be called invaluable, elevated versions. Elevated versions are few. If you continue to speak whenever you want and whatever you want, such words are not called elevated versions. Speak words that are necessary. Speak with tact and according to the time and place. Speak of that which brings benefit to the self and to others. The service of words and pure feelings should take place at the same time so that the combination of elevated words and pure feelings carries out the double task of understanding and experiencing.

Service Through Actions

Service through actions means to be part of a gathering, to come into relationship and connection with others. In your practical life, constantly be an embodiment of virtues. Be a visible sample and cooperate with others by easily donating virtues to them through your actions. Do not consider service through actions simply to be physical – to do cleaning and serving food, planning programs, and giving lectures. People are tired of listening. They now want to see the practical proof. Let your actions become a sample that make it simple for others. They are your brothers and sisters. They are part of the same family. Serve them with mercy from the heart.

ATTAINMENTS OF *RAJA YOGA*

Purifying the Soul

When impure gold is melted over a fire, all the alloy can be removed so that only the pure gold remains. Whereas some people walk over burning coals, your intellect goes to God in the fire of love. By remembering Me, you become pure, and all your sorrow and impurities are burned. I guarantee that if you remember Me, your sins of many births will be destroyed in that fire of *yoga*. I remove the rust that has been collected on you for birth after birth. All of that is burned, and you become pure gold!

Recharging the Battery of the Soul

I give a strong and powerful current, called *sakash*. This is the current of light and might. It is only through this current that the battery of your soul is recharged, that you gain strength to remove the alloy. You must practice receiving *sakash* and using it for transformation.

Reclaiming the Powers of the Soul

Through *yoga*, I will My powers to you, and you become complete with all powers, that is, no power is lacking. In your practical life, you are able to invoke from within yourself whichever power you need at any time for any circumstance.

THE POWER TO WITHDRAW is to merge all thoughts and to stabilize them in one pure thought, and with determination, to be in the awareness of the point form, the soul. It is the balance between being essenceful and being in the expansion.

THE POWER TO TOLERATE works well with the virtue of patience. It is the ability to see and respect the uniqueness of the other. It brings depth and maturity. To tolerate is to go into the depth of spiritual truths and emerge with the wisdom to have One strength and One support.

THE POWER TO COOPERATE grows out of the seed of love. To have the seed of the experience of spiritual, selfless love automatically leads to being cooperative through pure thoughts, pure feelings, and benevolent actions. The power of cooperation is very great. It brings closeness and builds strong relationships.

THE POWER TO ACCOMMODATE is to be in a stage of equanimity and to remain unaffected while being in different situations. To accommodate is to have a broad outlook with which to transform defects into virtues, and with pure and unlimited feelings to make a gathering powerful and united.

THE POWER TO DISCERN is to be stable in spiritual truths with a clean and clear understanding of truth and falsehood. To discern the physical aspects such as words and actions is a common matter, but to be able to discern thoughts, feelings, and vibrations is a spiritual power.

THE POWER TO JUDGE is for the scales of spiritual principles and spiritual love to have equal balance and for the pointer of the intellect to be absolutely still. To judge is to know right from wrong and to have the power to decide. To judge accurately the needs of others and to fulfill their spiritual rights requires being free from self-interest.

THE POWER TO FACE is to be fearless, cool, and calm on the inside and to be courageous, clear, and confident when facing external situations and obstacles. The power to face is first of all to have the realization of whether something is of benefit or loss and then, in facing the situation, to bring benefit.

THE POWER TO PACK UP is to have an easy and honest nature. It is the ability to sort out thoughts, feelings, words, and actions and only retain those that will strengthen the foundation. The power to pack up is to be light and powerful.

The eight powers are your spiritual arms that bring you victory on the field of action. Understand their strength and use them at the time of need.

Experiencing Contentment in Your Present Life

With constant remembrance, you experience pure contentment. Your stage ascends. At this time, I come and grant you the fruits of the efforts you made as a devotee. From the Copper Age onwards, you had been searching for Me for birth after birth. There are two fruits that I grant you: First is liberation, which means to experience peace and silence in the home, and second is liberation-in-life. There is no need to ask Me for anything. I Myself will give you everything you need. I keep My vision on all the souls. I have to benefit each and every one.

The true reward of studying and imbibing spiritual knowledge is that of liberation-in-life. Liberation-in-life is when both soul and body live with purity, peace, and happiness in a natural world where the elements of nature are in their perfect state of order, that is, in the Golden Age. I have come to cleanse you, the soul, and to re-emerge your Golden-Aged *sanskars*. However, you cannot live in anticipation of experiencing these *sanskars* in a future age. The future is created on the basis of the present. Make the effort to live a life of liberation now and to re-emerge your Golden-Aged *sanskars* now.

Your present life is the most valuable one. It is in this life that I teach you, and it is in this life that you make effort to follow the highest code of conduct.

BRINGING BENEFIT TO THE WORLD

This is the beneficial age, and you can be one who is a benefactor soul. A soul who brings benefit to the whole world is, first of all, complete with all treasures. Remain in your self-respect of being a benefactor soul. First there has to be benefit for the self, and together with that, benefit for others. The more effort you make individually to stay in remembrance, the more support you give to the world. Through the power of your *yoga*, the world becomes pure. It is a wonder how you purify the world with your *yoga*!

Every day, while in *yoga*, become the embodiment of the bestower of blessings for the world. Experience the combined form with Me, the World Benefactor, so that you, the bestowers of blessings, and I, the World Benefactor, are together. Stay in the combined form, and then, through the thoughts of your mind and through your attitude, you can spread the fragrance of those vibrations in the world. Each day, be like a fountain of a variety of elevated vibrations and spread those vibrations to all other souls. Sprinkle all souls with these qualities in the same way that water is sprinkled from a rose water sprinkler. Nowadays, there is a very bad odor of unclean thoughts within the world, and so cleanse the world of this odor and fill it with fragrance.

. . . The Father brings this lesson on Raja Yoga to a close. Raja Yoga, He says, is how you will learn to create and sustain an elevated awareness of yourself and others. As you learn to remain in the consciousness of yourself as a soul, a conscient point of light linked to Him, you will gain total mastery and authority. You will not need for Him to bring you more of the magical agent, He says. You will be the embodiment of all the powers and virtues that you once had, that He has.

"Manmanabhav," He says, "be Mine with your mind." He tells you that the practice of Raja Yoga is a way of remembering, and that with it you can return home with Him. To reclaim your lost kingdom, you must practice Raja Yoga at this time.

IMPLICATIONS FOR LIFE

The power of purity, accumulated over
a period of time, gives support and strength to
the world. You accumulate purity through the
power of silence. In silence, there should only be
the Father and you. In silence, the soul connects
to the Supreme Soul and draws spiritual power.
The current of light and might is transmitted
directly from the Supreme Soul to the soul, and
the battery of the soul is recharged.

NINE

THIS ONE: THE CHARIOT

*S*ince your last lesson, you have spent considerable time practicing what your
Father calls Raja Yoga. You have found that it does not seem to matter where
you sit to do this practice. After a few minutes, you are able to withdraw your
consciousness from the body you are in and stabilize yourself as the tiny point of light,
the tiny star in the forehead.

As that tiny star, you find you can leave the limitations of the Earth through your
awareness and experience the place He describes as your original home, the place where
you were with Him and all other souls. You find deep comfort in the atmosphere of peace
there and often become absorbed in that experience of peace to the exclusion of all other
awareness.

As you have been experimenting more, you find that He was right and that you do
not need to drink anything, or say, or chant anything as you had in your days on the
other side of the door when you were searching.

You are so absorbed in your thoughts that you do not hear Him walking toward
you. Suddenly you sense His presence and find that He is settling down next to you.
Your heart and your eyes rise up to greet Him.

He greets you with His heart and eyes as well, then after a few moments tells you *that this is the greeting of souls to one another: souls speak in the language of the eyes. This is called* drishti. *Our natural state, He tells you, is silence. He then smiles at you and asks whether your practice of Raja Yoga has raised new questions inside – about who this is who has come to meet you in a human form, but speaks to you of souls as eternal points of light, as tiny stars.*

He doesn't give you a chance to respond, but turns so He is facing you directly and looks closely into your eyes. You fix your eyes on Him and feel your natural love for Him well up inside of you. He smiles and briefly puts the tip of His finger on your forehead. Inside your body, in the center of your forehead, He says, you are residing – as if in the seat of a chariot. You, the soul, are guiding the body you are in, and as you develop mastery through your practice of Raja Yoga, you will find your ability to easily guide your chariot increasing until you are barely aware of the chariot and completely aware of yourself as a being of light.

He then lifts His finger to His own forehead and touches it briefly. Inside of this chariot, He says, there are two souls. The one that took this body in the womb, and a second soul who entered after this chariot was in the final stages of his life. The second soul is the One who is teaching you, the One who is giving you love through the eyes of this chariot, the One who is your Father and the Father of all souls. He pauses to allow time for you to absorb what He is telling you.

You lean closer to Him and look deeply into His eyes. His eyes are fixed on you, and you feel as if the nectar from the magical potion is pouring into you. Your love for Him is absolute. Although you are quite sure you had never seen this physical body before you passed through the door to the Confluence Age, you recognize His eyes and the feeling of closeness and unbounded love each time you are with Him. You, at last, understand the true meaning of the language of the eyes.

He explains that of all of the mysteries of the known and unknown world, this mystery of the true identity of souls and the knowledge of how souls can reclaim their vast inheritance and be reunited with the Supreme Soul, their Beloved, is the most sacred. In a degraded and exhausted world, it would not have been possible for Him to find you and teach you if He couldn't meet you in a body and speak to you with a voice, so He has taken this body on loan.

Your eyes leave His and roam quietly over the face and body of this most fortunate chariot, the one who is carrying your Father, the Father of all souls. While you have grown fond of the physical presence over the time of your study, it is an ordinary body,

and you wonder how it was that this one was chosen. Your eyes return to His.

Guessing your thoughts, He continues. Each of you souls has a special role to play. In all of the drama of the world, no one else can play the role you play. Your specialties make you uniquely suited to play that part. Your destiny placed you in exactly the right place for each act of the drama. This one whom He has entered has this unique part to play. He is an experienced soul who has lived the full spectrum of life, and he is perfectly suited to play this part. His eyes, his voice, his arms are on loan to the Father of souls. Your Father tells you that His eternal name is Shiva, *and that it means benefactor. He has given the name of* Brahma *to the one whose body is on loan.*

It seems to you that the discovery you have made in your Confluence-Aged study is that nothing is as it appears to be: that the outer and visible world of matter is just the skin of the real, eternal world, and that the unlimited truth of the world dwells inside of that skin. It is not your body that is you, but the tiny star inside the body that is your true self. It is not the bottle or even the magical potion inside the bottle that gives you power, but the invisible stream of love connecting you to the Supreme. And now, you understand that it is not the tall form of this physical person who met you to teach you, but the brilliant living Seed within this form who is teaching you and planting the sapling of the new world.

You look at Him, you, the soul, linking to the invisible third eye in the center of the forehead of this very fortunate chariot, and you signal your understanding.

He continues to explain . . .

Teachings

in the world knows that

the Supreme Father, the Supreme Soul, sits in this one's body and gives knowledge. I enter this one's ordinary body. I take the support of this body. Whatever actions I perform, I perform them through this one, or I inspire him to perform them.

When I enter into the body of this human being, I sit in the center of the forehead next to the human soul. I am a guest. I enter and leave at My own will. Once I receive the organs, I become the Master of this body, and I begin to speak through the organs.

I enter with the specific aim to speak knowledge, and I remain totally detached. I come into sound so that I can take everyone beyond sound.

I come into the corporeal world into a corporeal body so that I can make My children complete and perfect. Always keep this in your consciousness – that it is your incorporeal Father who has descended into the corporeal world, into a physical body, and who is speaking to you. I am the One who is teaching. This one does not teach. I am the One who is sitting in this one's body, his chariot, and teaching. I call him the "lucky chariot." I come in an incognito way to explain to My children. Listen to me with this understanding.

Your mind carefully turns over what your Father is telling you, and you wonder about the one whom He is calling the "lucky chariot." Who was this one who was deemed worthy of such an elevated role in this drama? Sensing that you want to know more about the chariot, your Father obliges:

This one whom I named Brahma did not know his own births. I adopted an old, experienced body. No one is as experienced as he is. Brahma's soul is as old as a *kalpa*. He has gone through the entire cycle from the very first birth in the Golden Age to the last birth in the Iron Age. His role is from the beginning to the end. He has within him experiences of the whole tree and so is very mature.

He was born in India at the end of the Iron Age, and his name was Lekhraj. He was a jeweler, a successful businessman of diamonds and precious jewels. He was a very strong devotee with a deep love for the truth. As a seeker of truth, he encountered many scholars whose advice he sought and respected. He lived with his family in a community in which he was highly regarded. He was an ordinary human being fulfilling his duties and responsibilities with honesty and love.

When I incarnated, it is with this one that I made contact. I entered his life in his age of retirement to grant him the fruits of his devotion. This auspicious moment of our meeting is called the confluence.

You wonder what it must have been like for this man Lekhraj to have had the Supreme Soul enter his body. The One who has been called the Ocean of Love, the Ocean of Knowledge, must have given this ordinary one such an experience! Your Father guesses your thoughts . . .

Brahma was amazed . . .

Then He pauses briefly and seems to turn over the organs of the instrument to Brahma to tell of his own experience. The voice that speaks is the same, but the one who is speaking is the human being who you now understand is "the host":

"I had a vision in which Father Shiva said, 'Remember Me, and all your sins will be destroyed.' This was something new for me. Then Father Shiva gave me a vision of establishment of a new world and destruction of the old world. At that time, I did not have full understanding of what the Father was explaining. I just had the feeling that there was some unique power that had entered me. At night, when I was sleeping, I felt so light. It was as if I was flying. However, I did not understand the depth of anything.

"After that Almighty Power entered me, unusual things began to happen. When I would look at people, some of them would have visions. The eyes of these people would close, and when I asked, 'What is happening?' they would reply that they saw paradise or that they saw a divine being. This was something that took me time to understand. I took leave from my business and went away to Benares to try and understand. I would sit for long hours in solitude thinking of the Father and what He was saying through me. I spent those days drawing and writing of the things that were being revealed to me. I did nothing else. Finally I understood that the Father was guiding me to do this in preparation for my role.

"When Father Shiva entered my body and showed me the scenes of the destruction of the old world, I realized that the old world was going to go through difficult times, and I began to think to myself that I should forget about this worldly business and just do spiritual business. Instead of dealing with perishable diamonds and jewels, I should now deal with the imperishable jewels of spiritual knowledge. When I was made to understand that I was to become a self-sovereign, I experienced happiness inside. Because of these realizations, I renounced everything. I understood that this was the right thing to do."

As you take in this amazing story, you reflect on your own story and how many times your mind has been pulled back to your old life on the other side of the door. This one truly seemed the perfect choice for this unique role. You wonder if you would have had the courage to leave your old life so suddenly and so completely. Guessing your thoughts, your Father speaks through what you now understand is the mouth of Brahma:

Brahma did not leave anything. He recognized the benefit and transformed everything. He surrendered the ego of the intellect and the dictates of his own mind and became the embodiment of success through the method of *Manmanabhav.* He gave his wealth as the seed for world service with the faith that this giving was not giving, but was a means to receiving multimillionfold by touching the lives of millions. He fulfilled the responsibility to all of his physical relationships by transforming them with soul-conscious love. He did not think about what would happen or how it would happen. In a second, according to the Father's elevated directions and as soon as the Father gave a signal, Brahma carried out the action and took the step. His each step of courage brought him the return of a hundredfold help from the Father. This is how he became constantly pure, cool, and a bestower of happiness with his body, mind, and wealth.

Brahma's thinking and acting were according to My directions. Because he was the instrument for this new knowledge, he had to face so much opposition from people. Yet, by having the awareness of his self-respect, the company of the Father, and determination, faith, and spirituality, he constantly remained unshakeable and immovable. He lived his life like a lotus flower – detached from the dirt of the water while at the same time loving to all. No matter what confronting situations came up in relation to his own family members or from souls within the community, neither in his thoughts nor in his dreams did he have any upheaval of doubt.

Though you wouldn't say it aloud to your Father, it seems that at least in some ways Brahma must have had it easier than you and other students. It must be easy to remember the Father when He is sharing your body with you! No sooner has the thought emerged in your mind than your Father clarifies the point.

Each one has a direct relationship with Me. Brahma is a human being doing intense meditation to purify himself. This one has to make the most effort. Although I have taken this body on loan, this one has to make effort to have remembrance. Many times Brahma said:

"Although Father Shiva is sitting right next to me, I am still unable to remember Him all the time. Sometimes I forget Him. I understand that He is with me, but I still have to remember Him in the way that others do. It is not that I can just remain content that He is with me anyway. No! Remembrance slips away again and again. This destination is very high, and I have to make great effort in this."

I continually said to Brahma: "Remember Me constantly, because you are the one to whom all the storms will come first as tests. Otherwise, how could you explain to others how to use knowledge and remembrance to gain victory? You will be tested by all storms first."

We play a wonderful part together. However, the Almighty strength is Mine alone, not Brahma's. The body belongs to Brahma, and so whatever settlement of *karma* there is, this has to be dealt with by Brahma himself. It is not possible for Me to give special blessings to this one. This one too has to make effort for himself. These are his *karmic* accounts that he has to settle. Everyone has to settle all their *karmic* accounts with knowledge and *yoga*. That is the law. There is no question of blessings in that.

But what about Brahma's experience as a student, you wonder? He was the very first student in this "school for souls." Did the knowledge somehow travel inside of his head from the Teacher soul to the student soul so that he could instantly know things he hadn't known before? Again, the Father interjects.

I was teaching, and Brahma was also studying along with the rest of the children. He used to say:

"I too am a student, and I also have to pay attention to this study. When Father Shiva is sitting next to me in my body, I too listen to Him. When He is telling the children something, I too am listening to him . . ."

Brahma himself began listening to the knowledge at the age of 60. I gradually continued to speak knowledge a little at a time. I did not give all the knowledge at the same time. I gave a little knowledge every day. Brahma's special wonder was that although he was being used by the Father as an example for others to follow, he himself did not have any physical example to follow. Unshakeable faith and the Father's directions were his support. With this strength and support, he made the impossible possible. His intellect was always light and his mind was carefree. His slogan was, "This is the Father's responsibility, not mine."

I listen enrapt as the Father explains how this single human being, who is the point of entry to this wondrous Confluence Age, turned over his body and his life to God's task of establishing a new world. They were together more than 30 years in this one body, the Father steadily offering these jewels of knowledge of a rare truth hinted at in all scriptures, and Brahma, listening closely and serving as the model for all of those who would come afterward – those who would be magnetized to this mysterious school for souls and the establishment of a new world.

It is only from the Father that souls receive their unlimited inheritance. In the world, a child would receive an inheritance from the bodily father. Here souls receive their spiritual inheritance from Father Shiva. No one receives an inheritance from Brahma.

I sit in Brahma's body and give the children their unlimited inheritance of the treasures of knowledge, divine virtues, and spiritual powers. I re-establish the eternal relationship between the Supreme Soul and the souls. Because he has become the instrument through which I meet you, Brahma is also respectfully referred to as the "father of humanity." Even though the word *father* is used, Brahma is still part of the creation. The inheritance is received from the Creator, the One who is the Unlimited Father. The Father explains that it is not that Brahma claims his inheritance from the Father and gives it to others. No! Each one receives his or her inheritance directly from the Unlimited Father.

Brahma himself says to other students of *Raja Yoga*:

"You receive the unlimited sovereignty from that One. He is the greatest Father. Do not remember me! I do not have any property that you could receive. Remember the One from whom you are to receive the property. If you do not remember the Father, you automatically do not receive an unlimited inheritance. The Father also tells me, 'Consider yourself to be a soul and remember Me, and you will receive sovereignty over the world.'"

I teach you through the ordinary body of Brahma. I carry out establishment through him. I entered his body to give all My children unlimited peace and happiness. Although I give him the title of the "father of the people," I am the Supreme Father, the Supreme Soul, the Almighty Authority, and I give everything to the children. Some people think that Brahma is considered to be the Supreme Soul, but you now understand that this can never be so.

I, not this Brahma, attracted you, because I am ever-pure. He has the intoxication of being a long-lost, now-found child of Father Shiva. He understands that he is a beloved child of the Father.

He matched his thoughts and *sanskars* with Mine, and he moved along with easiness, respect, and love for others. His stage always remained stable and never fluctuated based on praise or defamation. He made special time in his daily timetable to practice staying in the *avyakt*, angelic stage. He did this through the practice of the bodiless stage, staying in the awareness of the point of light, the soul. The sign of coming close to his destination of becoming complete and perfect was the awareness of his complete *avyakt* form of the light of soul consciousness and of his future perfect form as a deity. The consciousness of the body totally merged, and the consciousness of these two forms emerged: the *avyakt*, angelic form, and the future deity form. This stage is called being equal to the Father. Being equal and being complete are the same thing.

His life became the living laboratory on the field of action for the experiments with completion and perfection. Brahma is the human instrument who embodied the purity and truth of the Father's teachings and directions and reached his *avyakt* stage of complete soul consciousness and his perfect stage of divinity. By the time of his changing from the corporeal form to the subtle, *avyakt* form, he had become incorporeal, egoless, and viceless. He is the example the Father uses to demonstrate the aim and objective of the teachings of *Raja Yoga*.

In the last moments of being in the physical body, what did Brahma do when he attained his *avyakt* stage? Like a bird, he flew away in one second. He flew away from the physical body in one second and reached the subtle region in his body of light.

His final conquest in the corporeal world was victory over death and the conquering of attachment. His final stage was the remembrance of One.

BRAHMA IN THE SUBTLE REGION

The time to go home is coming closer. However, before going to the incorporeal region, souls have to go home via another realm called the subtle region. Everyone has to meet there first, before going to the home. Souls meet with souls in their subtle bodies of light. Souls also meet with the Supreme Soul in a body of light. It is from this region that Father Shiva and child Brahma are currently serving.

It is only at this time out of the whole cycle that the subtle region emerges. With which power does the activity of the subtle region take place? In the Iron Age of the corporeal world, there are various forms of energy to make everything function. When electricity fails, you have many other means through which you can carry out your activities. You have your own generator to generate power for light.

What energy is used to make the activity of the subtle region function in the Confluence Age? The subtle region is the region of light, and so how would everything function in the region of light? What power is used to make everything function there? The activities of the subtle region function on the basis of the power of pure thoughts. Everything in this region functions through the power of the mind, the power of thought. When the Father switches on the power of thought, everything emerges.

Just as in the corporeal world, through the wireless, you are able to hear from far away all the news of the world that continues to happen, in the subtle region, because it is viceless and pure, the Father is able to keep a connection with the incorporeal and the corporeal worlds. This is why the Father is given the title, Lord of the Three

Worlds: corporeal, subtle, and incorporeal.

There is sound and movement in the corporeal world, whereas the incorporeal world is beyond sound, in total silence. In the subtle region there is no sound; there is only subtle movement based on pure thoughts. Just as you speak the language of words in the corporeal world, in the subtle region there is the heart-to-heart conversation through the power of divine *drishti*. This is called pure thoughts and pure feelings through the language of the eyes.

In order for thoughts and feelings to reach the subtle region, the power of remembrance has to be very deep and refined. The wire of the intellect has to be so powerful that no form of illusion, ignorance, or vice can cause interference in between.

At present, Brahma continues to sustain the Father's task of world transformation with the power of pure thoughts and is cooperating with the Father in the growth of world service. He serves the Father with his "chariot of light."

Through *avyakt* Brahma's body of light, I serve everyone from the subtle region in an unlimited way. I, the Incorporeal Being, do not have a physical or subtle form of My own. So I serve through the instrument of the subtle form of *avyakt* Brahma. I serve all souls at a subtle level.

Now Father Shiva and Brahma are in front of the children, working together at a fast speed in the subtle region. The speed of this subtle service is very fast, as it works outside the limitations of the physical body. This subtle service serves as a lift to elevate the children's efforts from a walking pace to a flying pace, to remove labor and tiredness, and to give zeal and enthusiasm.

From the subtle region, I look at you with subtle *drishti* through the eyes of *avyakt* Brahma, but I am the One who you remember. I am connecting to you through this one's subtle body of light, but I am the One with whom you have all relationships. In addition to remembering Me in the incorporeal world, you can also connect to Me in the subtle region at any time. You can be with Me for as long as you want, and you do not need an appointment. However, for this you need to pay attention to refining the purity of your thoughts and feelings.

THE *AVYAKT* STAGE

I am the Seed of the human world tree, and I have come to serve all souls of the tree. The cries of souls are becoming louder and louder daily as they call out for liberation from the different forms of pain and sorrow. They are tired of listening and tired of words. They want the experience. To give the experience of peace and spiritual power to such souls requires subtle service. Subtle service is done with the power of the mind from an *avyakt* stage of complete soul consciousness.

In the subtle region, there is the image of Brahma's body of light, and in this body there is Brahma's soul in its complete and perfect form. I also serve through this form of Brahma. I am so unlimited that I sustain you from the soul world as well as from the subtle region. Through the body of light of *avyakt* Brahma, I give you many different types of experiences to keep you entertained and interested. When I speak to you, it transcends words and is pleasing to your mind and brings sweetness to your soul.

What is the specialty of being in the *avyakt* stage? It is to have mastered the practice of detachment and to have the natural experience of being beyond — to experience the soul as bodiless, being separate from the body. This is called the complete stage of the pilgrimage of remembrance and the practical result of *yoga*.

Because he is *avyakt*, Brahma is easily able to experience *avyakt* bliss, *avyakt* love, and *avyakt* power. These are his subtle instruments of continued sustenance to the corporeal world, which he transmits through *sakash*. *Sakash* is spiritual light and might sent into the world through the power of the mind, giving the donation of peace and power to souls and matter.

Through *avyakt* Brahma, I give you the experience of what the *avyakt* stage is. You, in turn, can teach others what this stage is by living it through your corporeal body in a practical way. When you are in the *avyakt* stage and spirituality is filled in your every activity, you are full of impact. When others see your transformation, they are drawn to your *avyakt* attraction. Your practical life is the instrument with which to explain to people about this stage and subtle transformation. People are tired of listening to words, and because of this tiredness, they come into conflict with words. However, when they see the practical proof of your *avyakt* life, they will not have the courage to challenge you, rather you will give them strength and hope. You have the proof of *avyakt* Brahma, and others will have the proof of your life.

There is the saying, "The world is created through your vision." Let there be spirituality and divinity in your vision. Vision is called *drishti*. Your *drishti* should be such that the world changes. You should be able to see whatever you look at or whomever you look at with the vision of soul consciousness.

. . . His voice comes to a stop, and you sit together in silence. You now understand the mystery of this ephemeral world you have found yourself in and the magnetism of your Father's powerful vision which drew you here. Slowly He rises to His feet and motions for you to go for a walk with Him. As you walk along next to Him, you feel as if you are walking with your Friend, an equal, one in whom you can confide your inner thoughts and in whom you have total trust. He leads you down a path to the edge of a lake, and you both turn to walk along the lake. Across the lake is a village spilling down a hillside. It is all lit up and looks beautiful reflecting in the lake. You share this thought with Him.

He looks up at the village and back at you. He tells you that it is only from a distance that this village looks beautiful – that if you were to enter the village, you would find that its streets and residents are in the throes of the struggles with ravan *and the confusion of* maya. *But there is a place, He tells you, not too far from here where a model of paradise is being created.*

With this He has your attention. If there were a living model of paradise, then it would be easier to see the eternal virtues and powers alive in the world of matter. You tell Him that you want to see this model of paradise.

IMPLICATIONS FOR LIFE

In the subtle region there is no sound; there is only subtle movement based on pure thoughts. Just as you speak the language of words in the corporeal world, in the subtle region there is the heart-to-heart conversation with the Father through the power of pure thoughts and pure feelings.

TEN

MADHUBAN: A MODEL OF PARADISE

Your formal lessons are over, but your Friend, who is also your Father, Teacher, and Guide, has promised to take you to see *Madhuban, the living model of paradise. You are to wait for Him next to the lake. While you wait, you move easily into soul consciousness and practice* Raja Yoga. *In moments He appears in front of you, and you both head down the road that begins at the lake, but after a while leaves the lake and wanders over the hilly terrain of a high desert. At this time of year it is lush, but you can tell that in many times of the year it must be quite dry. You pass villagers and children. Some are herding goats. Women are carrying immense bundles of sticks on their heads. He directs your attention up ahead to a gateway. He tells you that this is Madhuban, and the town nearby is Mt. Abu.*

You step with Him through the gateway into a courtyard where many gather around Him. He stops and greets them all with His eyes. They stand in silence and return His silent and loving greeting. After a few moments, He takes you to another place on the grounds where there is a small yellow hut. You both leave your shoes at the door and sit down inside the hut. He tells you that He has brought you to this place so that you can see the sapling of the new world tree that is being created . . .

Teachings

to Abu, and I will show you

a very sacred pilgrimage place. Come to Abu, and I will show you the place of My divine activities, the place from which I am creating peace in the world and granting everyone salvation. It is here that the Father changes the whole world of sorrow into a world of happiness. Everything that is happening in this place is incognito. This is the highest pilgrimage place of all. The reason why Mt. Abu is the greatest pilgrimage place is that the Supreme Father, the Supreme Soul, comes to this place and establishes heaven. A day will come when many will come to Mt. Abu looking for Madhuban, the place where the magical flute of knowledge, the *murli*, is being played.

They will all want to learn ancient *Raja Yoga*, the knowledge and practice that return all human beings and the world to their sovereignty. They will come looking for the One who plays the flute of knowledge that creates magic in souls. I do not play a bamboo flute. The incorporeal Father plays the flute of knowledge only in Madhuban, and the sweet sounds attract souls from far and wide.

After explaining all the knowledge, I bring you here to Madhuban. Come with Me, and I will show you a model of paradise. I will show you a model of how children study *Raja Yoga* at the Confluence Age and become self-sovereigns and masters of the world. I will show you a model of those who do intense *yoga*. I will show you the memorials of everything that actually happens in practice. The land is here for all time. Father Shiva is here. Child Brahma is also here, and so is the model of paradise.

THE STORY OF IMMORTALITY

Why do you come to Madhuban? Here, the Father comes personally and speaks to you. It is from this pilgrimage place that Father Shiva gives knowledge through child Brahma. When child Brahma was in his physical body, it was on this land that Father Shiva and child Brahma worked together. It is the field of action of child Brahma. You come here to Madhuban because you know that this is the land on which divine activities are performed. You come to meet the incorporeal Father and *avyakt* Brahma who continue to sustain the children.

You come to listen to the story of immortality from the Father. The Father purifies the impure by telling the story of immortality. I definitely have to tell it here on a mountaintop.

In telling the story of immortality, I remind the children of the immortal throne of the soul, which is the awareness of being a sovereign, a master. I give you the awareness of the intoxication of being a master and then seat you on the throne of My heart. I stabilize you in the highest position and say: Sweet, sweet, beloved children, listen to the story of immortality and remember your eternal fortune. Use your divine intellect to listen and experience with recognition every aspect of the story. Use your spiritual vision to see the images of the past, present, and future. The story of immortality gives to all children the experience of self-sovereignty. It reminds you of that which is immortal – the self, the Father, and the world drama.

THE LAND OF TRANSFORMATION

Madhuban is the land of transformation. It is your sweet home in the physical world and the asylum for the long-lost ones. The atmosphere here is created by the benevolent presence of the Father and the soul-conscious attitude of the children. This atmosphere creates the maximum impact in a practical way on whomever comes to Madhuban. It is the land of the Father's blessings, and so that is the main power that transforms the atmosphere.

As soon as you step onto the land, you experience the atmosphere of transformation. There is the experience of spiritual intoxication and also of the company of the truth. When coming into connection with every soul, there is the attitude of benefit, love, cooperation, selflessness, elevated thoughts, and pure feelings. This experience is so strong that there is not even the awareness of how day changes into night and night into day.

To step into Madhuban is to step away from the whole world. Madhuban is a small place in a corner of the world, but on arrival it is as if you have reached an even more elevated place than the Golden-Aged world. You experience happiness in a forest. You experience the dry mountains of the surrounding desert to be a world of happiness and as elevated as pure love. You experience your world to have changed.

Madhuban is the land of blessings, the powerful land, the land of elevated company, the land of easy transformation, and the land that enables you to experience all attainments. Coming to such a land, everyone experiences the fulfillment of all spiritual treasures. There is no lack of attainment in anything. Everyone feels the unlimited capacity to imbibe all the treasures received.

You leave this land having become great donors, instruments to donate to everyone these spiritual treasures and all attainments. You experience yourself to be a destroyer of obstacles and embodiment of solutions for all time. You become this not only for your own problems, but you also become the embodiment of solutions for the problems of other souls.

A SAFE SPACE

The sun of truth never sets in Madhuban. Madhuban gives light and might to everyone. It is a place that provides all with equal access to knowledge, love, and sustenance. Madhuban is a house of mirrors. No one experiences illusions here. The light of truth nurtures everyone and protects them from battles, attacks, conflicts, and difficulties. No one labors. Everyone is safe in the comfort of the Father's home. Everyone receives spiritual refreshment here. You realize that by coming here for only a short time, you can rest and be refreshed. Rest is to be the embodiment of peace, and refreshed is to be spiritually fulfilled.

This special Madhuban exists at the Confluence Age. You are now at the Confluence Age. You have renounced the Iron Age. Outside the gates of Madhuban is the Iron Age. Outside, there are all the mundane matters. This is why Madhuban is remembered as a safe space. Within this space children churn knowledge. You have the elevated company of each other. Your conversations are always about knowledge and spiritual experiences. Everyone takes back a special gift from Madhuban, which is the seat of the authority of all experiences. This gift keeps you safe wherever you go.

Madhuban has a double boundary. One is the atmosphere of the place itself. The other is that everyone stays within the boundary of *shrimat*, the supreme directions. So children are within the double boundary on this land. The stage of those who remain within this double boundary must be so elevated and free!

A FAMILY OF LONG-LOST CHILDREN

In Madhuban, you laugh, dance, and sing. You enjoy yourselves very much here. The Father is also pleased to see the children enjoying themselves. Love attracts everyone towards the Father. Madhuban attracts all the children because here you live practically as members of God's family. The Father considers all the children to be the decoration of Madhuban, His corporeal home. Children are the decoration of a home. There is sparkle and beauty in Madhuban because of the children. The Father is very pleased to see the splendor of the variety of children in Madhuban. Just as there are many connections of light from the physical powerhouse, so the Father is seeing the many beings of lights, souls who have come to the spiritual powerhouse of Madhuban.

You come personally in front of the Father, who makes children into the masters of the land of constant happiness. You now understand that there is a vast difference between listening to the Father from a distance and listening to Him personally. Here you come personally to be close to the Father and to listen directly to Him and experience the reality of what He is teaching.

SPECIALTIES OF THE RESIDENTS

To be a resident of Madhuban means to be a resident of a great and pure land. Since those who visit this land have a great fortune, imagine how great the fortune must be of those who live here! The residence of great souls is also remembered as a great place. Since those who visit here experience themselves to be great and have many different experiences within themselves, imagine what the experience of those who live here would be!

No matter where any of you come from, once you enter the gates of Madhuban, you are all residents of Madhuban. Therefore, all residents of Madhuban have easily become embodiments of remembrance. It is a sign of great fortune to become a resident of Madhuban, because to enter the gates of Madhuban means to attain a blessing for all time, the blessing of being stable and unshakeable.

Madhu means honey and *ban* means forest. The nature of Madhuban is of sweetness. And the freedom of the land is a natural detachment from all types of limitations. The residents of Madhuban are those who, with their sweetness, constantly make others sweet, and those who, with their own attitude of unlimited distaste for sorrow and bondages, inspire distaste in others for those things as well. This is the specialty of the residents of Madhuban – the extreme of sweetness in nature and the extreme of distaste in attitude.

Madhuban is a special stage. Madhuban means a great stage, and so those who play a part on the great stage must also be great. Every word that the residents of Madhuban utter is a pearl. They are not words, they are pearls. When they speak, it is as though there is a shower of pearls, not of words. There is the value of newness in every word. Every word conveys the experience of the vibrations of good wishes and pure feelings for the self and others. That is what is called sweetness.

CULTURE OF LOVE

The greatest sustenance is the love for spiritual knowledge. The other sustenance is of food prepared with love in remembrance of the Father. One is the sustenance for the soul, and the other is the sustenance for the body. There is also the sustenance of being with the family of a variety of brothers and sisters from all over the world. All three types of sustenance take place in Madhuban.

Madhuban is like an ocean of love. There is an unlimited flow of love from hearts that are big, generous, and open. It is the place where children are merged in the love of the Comforter of Hearts, and the Father, the Comforter of Hearts, is merged in the love of the children. It is love that gives the children spiritual birth, and it is love that sustains them on the journey of spiritual growth. In Madhuban, everything operates and is sustained by the power of love. Love removes labor and makes children free from worry, love enables them to experience the canopy of the hand of blessings over the self at every moment, and love gives them the experience of guaranteed victory in every action. In Madhuban, love transforms stones into diamonds and changes mountains of problems into mustard seeds. In this land of love, children become lost in love. Love is constantly radiated from the sparkle in the children's *drishti* and the beauty in their smile.

LIGHTHOUSE

Madhuban is the lighthouse and might-house. The light of the lighthouse falls on all souls. To whatever extent souls are able to receive the light of vibrations, to that extent they consider Madhuban to be somewhere unique. The impact of the power of Madhuban is felt as something special happening in the world. People of the world are affected by the waves generated in this land. The vibrations of Madhuban are spreading everywhere.

The day will come when everyone will come to know that the Father, the Ocean of Knowledge, has come to fill their aprons with the imperishable jewels of knowledge. At that time, so many children will come, do not even ask! You know that these teachings of *Raja Yoga* are very easy to understand. When people come to know that here they can receive the jewels of knowledge which will make their lives simple and elevated, they will continue to come. People will tell one another of this place.

They will be queuing from Abu Road to set foot on the sacred land on the mountaintop!

. . . Your Father asks if you are pleased that the formal part of your study is over. You are, of course, grateful for all you have learned, but you feel a small wave of the concern you felt on the very first day you arrived in this mysterious space and time – wondering if it is possible that you could lose your access to this Confluence Age and find yourself back in the Iron Age with no idea where the doorway was through which you entered.

He tells you that this is all in your hands – that if you follow shrimat *and practice Raja Yoga as a part of your daily life, then you will find yourself in His constant companionship, and you will find the world around you cooperating with you.*

But what about ravan, *you ask. Even the village you passed by this morning is deep in the throes of the vices of* ravan *and the illusion of* maya. *Surely as you return to your place in the world, you will encounter these forces.*

Yes, He says, the Iron Age is the age of ravan, *and most of the world is heavy with the burdens of their past* karmas *and their* karmic *bondages. The magic of the Confluence Age is that it exists in the midst of the Iron Age and is virtually invisible to those in that age. Not all the souls who are a part of the roots of this tree reside here in Madhuban, He says, but many of them come here to receive sustenance, to study, and to strengthen their practice of Raja Yoga. Then they return to their own fields of service around the world, just as you will now return to yours.*

Your heart stops for a moment. You have not been thinking about returning to your ordinary life and tell Him that. You were thinking of staying here with Him and with the others.

He smiles and looks at you with eyes filled with love. You do not need to remain here in order to be with Him, He reminds you. Besides, you have work to do in the world.

For a moment you are confused. Why is He urging you to go back to your ordinary work in the world? It was, after all, your lack of satisfaction with that life and that work that led you to search for the truth that you have found with Him.

As usual, He picks up your thoughts and explains. That is not the work to which He was referring, He says, although you can continue with that work in order to support yourself.

The work we are all engaged in now is the transformation of the world. While ravan *and* maya *are very powerful forces, they diminish in the presence of the power of truth. You and the others here are becoming self-sovereigns. As you transform your mind, your intellect, and your* sanskars, *the vibrations that you emanate become more elevated; your subtle powers become more refined; and you find you can see the past, the present, and the future at once. At a certain point, this force of truth and light will conquer the forces of falsehood, and the entire world will transform. Until that time, your task is to dedicate yourself to perfecting yourself and helping others who are searching for this truth. Your task is to bring comfort and hope to the world.*

You sit in stillness for a few moments and absorb this understanding. These words of His seem to shine a light on the only remaining part of your intellect where there was still a lack of understanding. Now you find you have no more questions. You realize that for the first time since you entered the Confluence Age and felt His presence that you no longer see with double vision. Your understanding of the truth is planted deep within you, giving you clear and elevated vision.

You listen inside for an instant and know what you must do. It is time to return to the world so that the world can return to its original pure state. You look at your Friend one last time and thank Him silently with your eyes before you stand up to begin your return journey. You know that you will return to Madhuban in the future to take the sustenance of this magical place, and you know that you never need to be away from Him for even a moment. You step through the door, slip on your shoes, and begin to make your way back to the world and the elevated task that lies ahead.

IMPLICATIONS FOR LIFE

Madhuban is the lighthouse and might-house.

The light of the lighthouse falls on all souls.

People of the world are affected by the waves

generated in this land. The vibrations of

Madhuban are spreading everywhere.

Catch the vibrations from Madhuban!

To My sweetest, beloved, long-lost and now-found children,

love and remembrances

from your Mother, your Father.

The Spiritual Father says namaste *to the spiritual children.*

AFTERWORD

I do not remember a time when I was not interested in finding God and the truth. The daughter and granddaughter of very devout Sindhis, I was raised in an area of India that is now in Pakistan. With my father and grandfather I studied the Hindu scriptures, which resulted in my having a lot of love for God and a deep desire to know who God is. But when I read the stories in the scriptures, the experience left me feeling confused and unclear as to who God is, who I am, and from where we all originally came. After reading the *Bhagawad Gita*, I found myself grappling with the question, in my own life, what should I do? Should I become a housewife? Should I become a leader? Should I become a spiritual *guru*? Should I become someone's follower?

In 1936, when I was 20 years old, I had an experience that instantly showed me the way forward. I was out walking with my father, when ahead of us, walking towards us, was Brahma Baba, who I knew from social settings in the past. He was a highly respected diamond merchant and jeweler and a frequent guest in the homes of the wealthiest and most influential people. I knew that he had recently come into some new knowledge and that those around him had begun to hold spiritual gatherings to be in his presence and take from this new knowledge.

As he came closer to us, my vision of him became transfused with light. It was as if his face and body dissolved into light. This experience, though fleeting, moved me deeply, and I resolved to go myself to these gatherings. When I began attending these gatherings, I realized I was hearing knowledge that I had never read in any scripture or heard from any *guru*. The sound that kept coming in my mind was that these must be messages of the Supreme Soul. This knowledge cannot be coming from a human being; this one is telling me the truth. After so many visits to *gurus* and hearing so many scriptures, here finally was the crystal clarity of the truth about the most important knowledge in the universe – the soul, the Supreme Soul, the home of souls, the history of the world, everything.

He explained how the imperishable soul plays a part in a perishable body. He showed us that we can create a connection with the Supreme Soul and attain those qualities and powers that are imperishable. I would observe the way Brahma Baba would explain. Concepts that had been vague before and hard to grasp fell into place, giving me an understanding of the unfolding of time and the experience of the souls in time and of our relationship to the Supreme. Brahma Baba made it clear to all present that he, Brahma Baba, was not the Supreme Soul, but that the Supreme was using his body as a sort of chariot to give these truths to the souls of the world at this time.

There is a saying in Hindi: "You are my Mother, Father, Teacher, Guide, and Friend." As I came to know the Supreme Soul in these meetings, I came to feel myself in these relationships with Him. God in the relationship of a Mother makes me Hers and sustains me with love. God in the relationship of a Father makes me worthy. God in the relationship of a Teacher gives me knowledge and as a Guide, He tells me what to do. I was then able to understand what it means to become *satopradhan* – pure in the extreme and of the highest quality. However, together with this, one thought still persisted: How can I imbibe this elevated knowledge? Then God in the relationship of my Friend offered His friendship and made it easy for me. My student life became easy and enjoyable, and I earned tremendous spiritual income. My Teacher was also my Friend, and this made my studies easy.

My intellect stopped searching and became still and stable in knowing the truths that were being told to me. I never used my intellect in thinking and writing too much. My intellect became calm, quiet, and peaceful, and elevated thoughts began to come naturally into my mind. These elevated thoughts naturally became my actions. The basis of my elevated thoughts and actions was the knowledge of who I am, who God is, and the practice of having a connection, having *yoga* with God. I had the clear understanding of what life is and realized that knowledge is very important to the practice of *yoga*.

One of the understandings I gained in this study was about the meaning of the present time of the Confluence Age – the transition between the Iron Age, which is my past, and the Golden Age, which is my future. It is in this transitional period that I have the chance to become a self-sovereign, a divine being. This is the time when the study of the real *Raja Yoga* takes place. Included in *Raja Yoga* is *karma yoga*. This means that I do not have to renounce action in order to have *yoga*.

I am being taught how to perform elevated actions and at the same time to incinerate my *karmic* account of bad actions with the practice of *yoga*. Spiritual power accumulates in the soul as the impressions on the soul of bad actions are incinerated. This growing spiritual power enables me to perform elevated actions. I became very clear about the difference between an elevated action and a bad action. God as my Friend always reminds me that for me to make this continuous progress, I need courage. The courage of the child draws help from the Father.

As I maintain courage, my understanding deepens. I understand in the deepest way what the truth is, what *dharma* – or religion – is, what *yoga* is, what the original form of the soul is, and what the eternal form of the soul is. My increasing understanding of these deep aspects of knowledge makes elevated living practical. When I understand spiritual truths in a practical way, then I am able to practice them in my life. When the practical is clear, then I am able to practice that. It is the practical aspect of the study that caused Brahma Baba to call it easy *Raja Yoga* and makes the student into an easy *Raja Yogi*.

God forewarns me of the obstacles that I will encounter in my studies, and He gives me methods to remove each obstacle as I encounter it. This is the path to self-sovereignty. A self-sovereign is someone whom God Himself made His child and then taught him or her to be a master of the self. God told me this at the moment of my spiritual birth – that to be a self-sovereign is my birthright. To rule myself I need peace, love, happiness, purity, and the power of truth. These innate qualities are my spiritual rights, the rights I claim from God at the time of my spiritual birth. This is the common sense, basic understanding that I need to have if I am to become a self-sovereign.

Over the long history of the soul, through time, we lose the memory of our true birth, our true Parent, and our birthrights. When I was defeated by my sense organs, I lost my connection to these spiritual rights. Whatever I study, learn, practice, and make part of my practical life is my experience. Through this process, I reclaim spiritual rights as my own, and these can naturally be shared with others in the form of attainments. I serve others with the attainments of what I have studied. My life is the proof of my spiritual progress with this study. Just to be in the presence of someone who is making this deep spiritual effort and gaining spiritual attainments touches and transforms something in others.

Over the years of my study, I had the distinct feeling that God inspired me to study in order to serve people from every corner of the world. So when I came to the West in the 1970s, I knew exactly what was needed in terms of sharing this knowledge with people from different traditions and cultures, and I witnessed the universal appeal of this knowledge. For every religion, for every human being, this knowledge is needed. This is the experience I have of world service. Whatever knowledge each one has received is exactly right for him or her. It is the exact message that they want to receive. The knowledge is received and stored in the memory bank, and at the right time it will be of use to them in a practical way. From the depths of my heart, I serve with the pure feelings that every single human being should understand spiritual truths.

It is important for human beings to know what the self is saying, what God is saying, and what time is saying. In the present situation of the world, what is it that needs to be done? What is our collective future? What is the path we need to walk on together?

Dadi Janki

Administrative Head
Brahma Kumaris World Spiritual University

The End . . .
and the Beginning

Look back and see the Iron Age.

Look forward and see the Golden Age.

Stay steady in the Confluence Age.

Glossary

A

atma: soul. The individual soul as distinguishable from the Supreme Soul, *paramatma*.

avyakt: not manifest or apparent. Very subtle energy that manifests in the form of pure, refined, spiritual light. *Avyakt* form can be referred to as angelic form.

B

Baba: Father, a term of endearment.

bliss: the exchange of pure joy – beyond the range of the senses – between the Supreme Soul and the soul. Supreme bliss is an experience that souls have in the exclusive company of the Father in a state of complete belonging.

brahm: The element of *brahm* is a region of golden-red divine light that fills the soul world. It is a place beyond the physical dimension of the sun, moon, and stars and is referred to as *nirvana*, or the sixth element of light.

bodiless stage: to be in the awareness of the point of light, the soul, and to experience being separate from the body while the soul is still in the body.

C

churn: to think about, ruminate, ponder, or cogitate upon points of spiritual knowledge. As a metaphor, to "churn" the "milk" of knowledge and extract the butter.

completion: entire, whole, full, e.g., the full moon. Every soul enters the world in its original stage of completion, totally pure, with no trace of gross or subtle vices.

Confluence Age: the age of transition. The most subtle and elevated of the great ages of humankind, the Confluence Age is a time of transformation and Divine intervention. This short time period, also known as the leap age, or Diamond Age, runs concurrently with the end of the Iron Age until the beginning of the Golden Age.

corporeal world: the physical world, the world of matter and material things, where there is sound and movement.

D

deities: human beings with divine virtues.

detached observer: A capacity that is highly desirable for a spiritual aspirant. One who is a detached observer is not only able to be a "witness," unaffected by external and internal influences, but is also able to observe situations while being fully aware of the subtle dynamics at play. The detached observer is able to see a particular situation and understand it in the full context of the principles of *karma*, the three aspects of time, and the accuracy of the drama of life.

dharamatma: *Dharam* means religion or righteousness, and *atma* means soul: a righteous soul.

dharma: religion. To give foundational support and to hold together in cohesion and unity. *Dharma* is the code of universal, spiritual laws that gives direction to life and brings it back to a state of order and unity.

drishti: sharing of vibrations through the physical eyes. In spiritual terms, the love and good wishes one soul has for another is conveyed through eye contact.

Dwapuryug: the age when duality begins. *Dwapuryug* is the third quarter of the world cycle, the Copper Age, when seeking and devotion start. This is the age when happiness is mixed with sorrow, purity with impurity, order with disorder, and truth with falsehood. Its duration is 1,250 years. The maximum number of births souls can take during this age is 21.

E

elevated attitude: a state of mind characterized by soul-conscious love, acceptance of others, and feelings of spiritual connection; a way of being that does not discriminate against others.

G

guru: a venerable, honored, learned, and wise person who is a teacher or spiritual guide.

I

incorporeal: not corporeal: having no material body or form. The incorporeal form is pure spiritual light.

incorporeal world: the *brahm* element of light, where the Supreme Soul resides and where souls reside in complete silence and peace, as tiny points of light.

K

kalpa: duration of 5,000 years, which is the period of time measuring one complete cycle of the world. A *kalpa* consists of the Golden, Silver, Copper, and Iron Ages, and within each of these ages there is a progressive decline through which the world passes. The Confluence Age is the highest and most auspicious age, and it is the meeting of the end of one *kalpa* and the beginning of a new *kalpa*.

Kaliyug: last of the four ages, the Iron Age, when the world reaches its most degraded stage. The world is in a state of total darkness, when happiness is replaced by sorrow. Its duration is 1,250 years. The maximum number of births taken in this age is 42.

karma: action – an act, deed, work, occupation, function.

karma yoga: performing action in soul consciousness and in remembrance of God.

L

liberation: freedom, emancipation. Release of the soul from the body, and the experience of souls in the incorporeal world in a state of complete silence and peace.

liberation-in-life: to live a life of freedom. To be free from all bondages that cause pain and sorrow and to live a life of peace and happiness in the physical world.

M

Madhuban: *Madhu* is the Hindi word for honey, and *ban* is the Hindi word for forest; literally, the forest of honey. Madhuban is a spiritual pilgrimage place located in Mt. Abu, India.

Manmanabhav: Focus your mind on only One: Consider yourself to be a soul and remember God, the Supreme Soul.

mantra: a sacred word with the properties to evoke that which is original to the self.

maya: illusion, deceit, deception. The world as perceived by the senses, considered to be illusory. Infatuation with what is unreal. Subtle influence of the vices, caused by body consciousness. *Maya* often comes in the form of temptation.

murli: flute. The body of teachings known as *Raja Yoga* is conveyed orally, and it is referred to as the *murli*, or "flute of knowledge."

N

namaste: a greeting offered with respect: respectful salutation. The meaning is "I bow to you as a child of God."

P

perfection: prosperous, thriving, accomplished, abundantly endowed with. The soul in its state of perfection is filled with all spiritual powers and divine virtues and lives by the highest code of conduct.

R

raja: sovereign, king, master, ruler. The best and highest of its kind.

Raja Yoga: A practice of meditation undertaken to bring the soul into union with the Supreme Soul. *Raja Yoga* is also the study and practice of spiritual knowledge that results in a transformation of human awareness in relation to the self, God, and the world.

Raja Yogi: one who, through the spiritual link with the Supreme Being, aspires to the highest form of mastery over the physical senses and over thoughts, words, and actions.

rajopradhan: the state of the human soul at the time of duality, the state between soul consciousness and body consciousness, when purity is mixed with impurity, order with disorder, and truth with falsehood. *Rajopradhan* is the middling stage on a continuum between *satopradhan* (purity in the extreme) and *tamopradhan* (impurity in the extreme).

ravan: the five vices – lust, anger, attachment, ego, and greed. They are the base forces that dominate over the original virtues and powers in the soul during the *rajopradhan* and *tamopradhan* stages.

S

sakash: the current of spiritual light and might received directly from the Supreme Soul to souls and transmitted by souls to the world.

Sannyas Religion: founded in India by the prophet soul Shankaracharya. Those who belong to this religion are known as *Sannyasis*. *Sannyasis* are hermits who choose a life of renunciation and solitude by isolating themselves from the world with the aim of attaining liberation.

sanskars: An inborn power or faculty within the soul that determines the soul's individual and unique identity in terms of character, personality traits, talents, habits, and propensities.

satguru: literally, the true guide. *Satguru* is the title given to God as the only One who guides souls back home to the incorporeal world.

sato: The properties of truth, purity, and goodness are present, but not in their full state. On a continuum between *satopradhan* (purity in the extreme) and *tamopradhan* (impurity in the extreme), *sato* represents a place of partial purity.

satopradhan: the highest state of human existence and of the natural world, when total truth, purity, and goodness prevail.

Satyug: the age of truth and pristine virtue. It is the first of four ages, the Golden Age. It is also called the land of happiness, heaven, and paradise. Its duration is 1,250 years. The maximum number of births souls can take in *Satyug* is 8.

sattvic: purest matter in the form of food that the human being digests to support the highest and purest form of consciousness. A *sattvic* diet consists of totally vegetarian food cooked in God's remembrance.

Shiva: *Shiva* means the universally Benevolent One, the Supreme Benefactor, the Infinitesimal Point, the Seed of the human world tree. Qualities of Shiva as the Seed are auspiciousness and perfection.

Shiv Baba: Shiva, the Father.

shrimat: Supreme directions revealed by God, considered to carry auspicious omens.

soul consciousness: to be in the awareness of the self as a being of light seated in the center of the forehead and to interact with others in that consciousness.

subtle region: a realm of light between the incorporeal world and the corporeal world. The activities of the subtle region function through the power of pure thought and the power of pure feelings. The subtle region is also referred to as the angelic world.

T

T-junction intersection: where three roads meet. In India, such intersections are roads where frequent accidents occur. Therefore, devotees have created places there to perform worship as a means of protection.

tamopradhan: the lowest state of human existence and of the natural world; a state of complete darkness of ignorance, disorder, and unrighteousness.

Tretayug: the second of the four ages, the Silver Age, is called semi-heaven. There is a high degree of order, but it is not the highest; it is moderately less than *Satyug*. Its duration is 1,250 years. The maximum number of births souls can take in *Tretayug* is 12.

Y

yoga: yoke, link, or bond. Spiritual connection or union achieved through remembrance.

yogi: one who practices connection or union through remembrance.